Jane A

PRIDE

&

Prejudice

by Paula K. Parker

WordCrafts

WordCrafts Theatrical Press

Playwright's Notes

"It is a truth universally acknowledged, that a single man in possession of a good fortune, must be in want of a wife."

Thus opens **Pride and Prejudice** Miss Austen's second – and arguably most popular – novel - pitting the lovely but opinionated Lizzy Bennet against the handsome, wealthy, yet brooding and taciturn Mr. Fitzwilliam Darcy in a fencing match where reputations, family fortunes, and hearts are at stake.

A 2003 BBC poll placed **Pride and Prejudice** in the #2 spot in their list of the "UK's Best Loved Books," right behind Tolkien's "Lord of the Rings." A 2008 Australian survey pegged **Pride and Prejudice** on top of the "101 Best Books Ever Written." The novel is no less popular in the US, having spawned numerous film and stage adaptations including the 1940 version, starring Sir Laurence Olivier and Greer Garson, and the 2005 version with Matthew Macfadyen and Keira Knightley in her Oscar-nominated roll as Lizzy. The 1995 BBC mini-series with Colin Firth and Jennifer Ehle, popularized on PBS stations, is credited with spawning a renewed interest in Jane Austen among American teens. Amazingly, Jane Austen sold the copyright to **Pride and Prejudice** for the sum total of 110 Pounds Sterling, and never earned a penny in royalties.

I love history and literature and adapted this novel with an eye for authenticity and a determination to maintain the integrity of the original work. There is a tendency for some contemporary playwrights to inject their own values or agendas into the script when they adapt a popular novel for the stage or screen. But Jane Austen's work stands on its own. Lizzy, Mr. Darcy, Mrs. Bennet, and Mr. Wickham are delightful characters as Jane Austen created them, without trying to infect them with 21st Century proclivities.

I declined including set designs for this play, thus allowing theaters to accommodate the sets for their stage. **Pride and Prejudice** is a character-driven story and as such, works well with a minimalist set of a few chairs and table.

I have also intentionally kept stage directions to a minimum, preferring instead to allow the director freedom to direct the play.

Paula K. Parker

Characters (In Order of Appearance)

Mr. Bennet:	an older gentleman
Jane Bennet:	the eldest daughter
Elizabeth Bennet:	the second daughter
Mary Bennet:	the third daughter
Kitty Bennet:	the fourth daughter
Lydia Bennet:	the fifth daughter
Mrs. Bennet:	wife and mother
Sir William Lucas:	local squire
Maria Lucas:	youngest daughter
Charlotte Lucas:	eldest daughter
Mr. Bingley:	a wealthy young man
Mrs. Hurst:	his married sister
Mr. Hurst:	her husband
Miss Bingley:	his unmarried sister
Mr. Darcy:	his wealthy friend
Hill:	the Bennet's maid
Footman:	at Netherfield
Mr. Collins:	relative to the Bennets, a clergyman
Mr. Denny:	young soldier
Mr. Wickham:	young soldier
Lady Catherine DeBourgh:	patron of Mr. Collins and Mr. Darcy's aunt
Colonel Fitzwilliam:	Mr. Darcy's relative
Mr. Gardiner:	Mrs. Bennet's brother
Mrs. Gardiner:	his wife
Mrs. Reynolds:	housekeeper at Pemberley
Maid:	at the inn
Georgiana Darcy:	Mr. Darcy's sister

ACT I

Scene 1

SETTING: The Bennet's parlor.

AT RISE: **MR. BENNET** is sitting in his chair, reading a paper and the Bennet girls are seated around the room, doing needlework, reading, or decorating a hat. **MRS. BENNET** bursts through the door, excited.

MRS. BENNET
My dear Mr. Bennet! Have you heard? Netherfield Park is let at last!

(Excited comments among the girls. **MR. BENNET** continues to read his paper.)

MR. BENNET
I have not heard.

MRS. BENNET
But it is, for Lady Lucas has told me all about it.

(**MR. BENNET** makes no answer.)

MRS. BENNET
Do not you want to know who has taken it?

MR. BENNET
(Lowers his paper.)
You want to tell me, and I have no objection to hearing it.

MRS. BENNET
Why, my dear, you must know, Lady Lucas says that

Netherfield is taken by a young man of large fortune. He came down on Monday to see the place, and was so much delighted with it, that he agreed to take possession before Michaelmas.

KITTY
What is his name?

MRS. BENNET
Bingley.

LYDIA
Is he married or single?

MRS. BENNET
Oh! Single to be sure! A single man of large fortune; four or five thousand a year.
(To **MR. BENNET**.)
What a fine thing for our girls!

MR. BENNET
How so? How can it affect them?

MRS. BENNET
My dear Mr. Bennet, how can you be so tiresome? You must know that I am thinking of his marrying one of them.

ELIZABETH
(To **JANE**.)
It is a truth universally acknowledged, that a single man in possession of a good fortune must be in want of a wife.

MRS. BENNET
(Overhearing)
Yes, indeed.

MR. BENNET
Is that his design in settling here?

MRS. BENNET
Design! Nonsense, how can you talk so! But it is very likely that he may fall in love with one of them, and therefore you must visit him.

MR. BENNET
(Goes back to his paper)
I see no occasion for that. You and the girls may go, or you may send them by themselves, which perhaps will be still better; for, as you are as handsome as any of them, Mr. Bingley might like you the best.

MRS. BENNET
But, my dear, you must indeed go and see Mr. Bingley when he comes into the neighborhood; for it will be impossible for us to visit him, if you do not.

MR. BENNET
You are over-scrupulous, surely. I dare say Mr. Bingley will be very glad to see you; and I will send a few lines by you to assure him of my hearty consent to his marrying which ever he chooses of the girls. They are all silly and ignorant like other girls, although Lizzy has more quickness of mind than her sisters.

MRS. BENNET
(Sits, much put out.)
Mr. Bennet, you take delight in vexing me. You have no compassion on my poor nerves.

MR. BENNET
You mistake me, my dear. I have a high respect for your nerves. They have been my old friends these twenty years.

MRS. BENNET
You do not know what I suffer.

MR. BENNET
But I hope you will get over it, and live to see many young men of four thousand a year come into the neighborhood.

MRS. BENNET
It will be no use to us if twenty such should come, since you will not visit them.

MR. BENNET
Depend upon it, my dear, that when there are twenty, I will visit them all.

LYDIA
(Holding up the hat she's working on.)
Kitty, do you not think this is a dreadful hat?

KITTY
I'm sure Mr. Bingley will like it.
(She begins coughing.)

MRS. BENNET
(Very perturbed.)
We are not in a way to know what Mr. Bingley likes, since we are not to visit.

ELIZABETH
But you forget, Mama, that we shall meet him at the assemblies.

MRS. BENNET
Assemblies! That is something more; Lady Lucas said that Mr. Bingley means to be at the next assembly, with a large party.

LYDIA
How many is in the party, Mama?

MRS. BENNET
Lady Lucas said twelve ladies and seven gentlemen.

ELIZABETH
Too many ladies, not enough men.

LYDIA
Makes for uneven dancing partners.

JANE
When is the next ball to be, Lizzy?

ELIZABETH
To-morrow fortnight.

MRS. BENNET
Don't keep coughing so, Kitty, for heaven's sake! Have a little
compassion for my nerves!

KITTY
I do not cough for my own amusement.

MARY
I do hope that Mr. Bingley is a sensible man and not always
thinking of his own amusement.

MRS. BENNET
I am sick of Mr. Bingley.

MR. BENNET
I am sorry to hear that. If I had known as much this morning,
I certainly would not have called on him. As I have actually
paid the visit, we cannot escape the acquaintance now.

(General excitement among the Bennet
ladies.)

MRS. BENNET

What an excellent father you have girls! And it is such a good
joke, too, Mr. Bennet, that you should have gone this
morning, and never said a word about it till now.

MR. BENNET

(Folds his paper, stands up, and tucks paper
under his arm.)

Now, Kitty, you may cough as much as you choose.

(**MR. BENNET** exits while the women are
still fluttering.)

(BLACKOUT)

ACT I

Scene 2

SETTING: The Assembly Hall.

AT RISE: Ladies and Gentlemen are mingling and talking while the musicians warm up [offstage]. The Lucases are already present, when the Bennet ladies arrive. **LYDIA** and **KITTY** meet **MARIA** and move off to whisper in the corner, **MARY** follows **MRS. BENNET**, who finds a place to sit, while **JANE** and **ELIZABETH** meet **CHARLOTTE**.

CHARLOTTE
Jane, Elizabeth. At last you are come.

ELIZABETH
Hello Charlotte, Yes, we are late. Lydia could not decide how to wear her hair.

JANE
I do hope we have not inconvenienced anyone?

CHARLOTTE
No, indeed you have not. My mother has been most anxious to speak to your mother, since she has learned more about the party at Netherfield.

ELIZABETH
Indeed? Has the number of ladies grown whilst the men reduced?

JANE
That would be unfortunate.

CHARLOTTE

My mother learned from my father that Mr. Bingley is
bringing two ladies and two gentlemen.
Ah...you can see for yourself, as they are just arriving.

> (**MR. BINGLEY, MR. DARCY, MISS
> BINGLEY, MRS. HURST** and **MR. HURST**
> enter. **SIR WILLIAM** approaches **MR.
> BINGLEY**, who introduces him to his party.
> They are too far away from the girls for them
> to overhear.)

JANE

Do you know who they are, Charlotte?

CHARLOTTE

The one greeting my father is Mr. Bingley.

JANE

He has a nice smile.

CHARLOTTE

The ladies are Mr. Bingley's sisters. One of the gentlemen is
Mr. Hurst, who is married to Mr. Bingley's sister.

ELIZABETH
> (Indicates **MR. DARCY**.)

Is that he?

CHARLOTTE

No, the other gentleman.

ELIZABETH

Better and better.

CHARLOTTE

The gentleman speaking to my father now is Mr. Darcy. He is, as I understand, one of Mr. Bingley's closest friends.

> (**MRS. BENNET** comes bustling up, all excited.)

MRS. BENNET

Girls, girls! I just had it from Lady Lucas, that Mr. Bingley's friend, Mr. Darcy, is worth a vast fortune.

> (An exaggerated whisper.)

Ten thousand a year! He owns a house in town and a country estate in Derbyshire known as Pemberley.

> (Notices that **SIR WILLIAM** is leading the Netherfield party their way.)

Shhh...girls. They are coming this way.

> (Pretends to be looking at something else until the party arrives.)

SIR WILLIAM

Ah, Mrs. Bennet. May I present to you Mr. Bingley? He is newly come to Hertfordshire.

> (They curtsy/bow.)

And these are two of Mrs. Bennet's daughters, Miss Jane Bennet and Miss Elizabeth Bennet.

> (They curtsey/bow.)

MR. BINGLEY

How do you do, Mrs. Bennet? May I present to you my sisters, Miss Caroline Bingley, Mrs. Hurst, her husband, Mr. Hurst, and my friend Mr. Darcy.

> (Ad lib greetings with curtsies/bows. The music starts.)

MR. DARCY

Miss Bingley, would you do me the honor of this dance?

MR. BINGLEY

Miss Bennet, would you do me the honor of this dance?

JANE

I thank you sir, yes.

> (They cross the floor to begin dancing.
> **ELIZABETH** sits to watch. It is obvious
> the ladies and gentlemen from Netherfield are
> elegant dancers. When the music ends, **MR.
> DARCY** returns **MISS BINGLEY** to her
> sister. **MISS BINGLEY** is asked to dance by
> **SIR WILLIAM. MR. BINGLEY** returns
> **JANE** to her mother and then approaches
> **MR. DARCY** who is standing by the wall,
> near where **ELIZABETH** is sitting.)

MR. BINGLEY

Come, Darcy. I must have you dance. I hate to see you
standing about in this stupid manner.

MR. DARCY

I certainly shall not. I detest it, unless I am particularly
acquainted with my partner. Your sisters are engaged, and
there is not another woman in the room whom it would not be
a punishment to me to stand up with.

MR. BINGLEY

I would not be so fastidious as you are for a kingdom. Upon
my honor, I have never met with so many pleasant girls in my
life, and there are several of them uncommonly pretty.

MR. DARCY

You were dancing with the only handsome girl in the room.

MR. BINGLEY

Oh, she is an angel; the most beautiful creature I have ever

beheld...
                    (Sees **ELIZABETH**.)
There is one of her sisters; she is very pretty.

MR. DARCY
She is tolerable; but not handsome enough to tempt me. You
had better return to your partner and enjoy her smiles, for
you are wasting your time with me.

(BLACKOUT)

ACT I

Scene 3

SETTING: The Bennet's parlor.

AT RISE: Everyone but **JANE** is present.
ELIZABETH is down stage, looking out of the window.

KITTY
Lydia and I danced every dance at the last two balls.

LYDIA
And Mary danced none.

MARY
I care not for such things. I was quite content to discuss music with Sir William and Lady Lucas.

MRS. BENNET
Oh, my dear Mr. Bennet, since Mr. Bingley and his party have arrived in the neighborhood, we have had the most delightful balls. I wish you had been at the last dance. Jane was most admired. Everybody said how well she and Mr. Bingley look when they dance. Only think of *that*, my dear.

ELIZABETH
Jane was very much flattered by his attentions.

MRS. BENNET
We are all quite delighted with him. He is so excessively handsome. And his sisters are charming women. Their dresses were quite elegant. I daresay the lace on Mrs. Hurst's gown...

MR. BENNET
No lace, my dear. I care not to hear a description of it. Well, Lizzy, what say you? What of Mr. Bingley's friend I hear tell of?

MRS. BENNET
Mr. Darcy! What a rude, disagreeable man. Quite proud and vain.

MARY
Pride is a very common failing. Vanity and pride are different things, though the words are often used synonymously. Pride relates to our opinion of ourselves; vanity to what we would have others think of us.

(Everyone looks at her a moment.)

MRS. BENNET
Well, proud or vain, I don't like the man. He slighted Lizzy.

MR. BENNET
What? Slighted my Lizzy?

ELIZABETH
Do not worry, Papa. For my part, I cared not for him.

MRS. BENNET
Another time, Lizzy, I would not dance with *him*, if I were you.

MR. BENNET
I must agree.

ELIZABETH
Do not worry. I may safely promise you never to dance with Mr. Darcy.

LYDIA
Uncle Philips said the militia is to remain in Meryton for the whole winter.

KITTY
Yesterday our Aunt Philips told us that Colonel Forester is considering throwing a ball soon. He says his officers need time spent in polite company.

LYDIA
I would be glad to spend time in their company.
>   (Giggles.)

KITTY
I would be glad to spend time with any man wearing regimentals.
>   (Giggles.)

Now that the rain has stopped, let us walk to Meryton and see if we can meet any of them.

MR. BENNET
Mrs. Bennet, I think we may congratulate ourselves that here sit two of the silliest girls in the country.

ELIZABETH
Mama, I am concerned about Jane.

MRS. BENNET
The invitation yesterday from Miss Bingley to join her and Mrs. Hurst for luncheon was too good an opportunity to pass. The gentlemen were out hunting and if Jane had gone in the carriage, she might have missed seeing Mr. Bingley altogether; but if she went by horseback to Netherfield and it rained, she would be invited to stay the night. As it did rain, I was right in my thinking and - if the rain should return - she might stay yet another night.

(**HILL** enters with a note. She curtsies.)

HILL
It's for Miss Elizabeth, Sir. From Miss Jane.
>(Hands the letter to **ELIZABETH** and exits.)

ELIZABETH
>(Opens the letter and reads aloud.)

My dearest Lizzy, I find myself very unwell this morning, which I suppose is to be imputed to my getting wet yesterday. My kind friends will not hear of my returning home till I am better and, excepting for a sore throat and headache, there is not much the matter with me. Your loving sister, Jane.

MR. BENNET
>(To **MRS. BENNET**.)

Well, my dear, if your daughter should die of a dangerous illness, it would be a comfort to know that it was all in pursuit of Mr. Bingley and under your orders.

MRS. BENNET
Oh! People do not die of little trifling colds. She will be taken good care of.

ELIZABETH
Father, I should like to go to Jane.

MR. BENNET
Is this a hint to send for the carriage?

ELIZABETH
No, indeed, I shall walk. The distance is nothing, only three miles, I shall be back by dinner.

MRS. BENNET
Walk! How can you be so silly as to think of such a thing, in all this dirt! You will not be fit to be seen when you get there.

ELIZABETH
I shall be very fit to see Jane – which is all I want.

(BLACKOUT)

ACT I

Scene 4

SETTING: A parlor at Netherfield.

AT RISE: **MR. HURST** is sleeping in a chair,
MR. BINGLEY is writing a letter and **MISS
BINGLEY** and **MRS. HURST** are looking at a
magazine. **MR. DARCY** has a book opened, but is not
looking at it. Instead, he is staring off, with a pensive
expression. After a moment, **MISS BINGLEY** crosses
to **MR. DARCY**.

MISS BINGLEY
I can guess what you are thinking.

MR. DARCY
I should imagine not.

MISS BINGLEY
You are thinking how insupportable it would be to pass many
days in this neighborhood.

MR. DARCY
My mind has been more agreeably engaged, I assure you. I
have been meditating on the very great pleasure a pair of fine
eyes in the face of a pretty woman can bestow.

MISS BINGLEY
                (Brightens, thinking he is talking about her.)
And who might this be that caught your attention?

MR. DARCY
Miss Elizabeth Bennet.

MISS BINGLEY

Miss Elizabeth Bennet? I am all astonishment. When pray, am I to wish you joy?

(**FOOTMAN** enters.)

FOOTMAN

Miss Elizabeth Bennet.

(**ELIZABETH** enters, they all stand and curtsy/bow. **MR. BINGLEY** crosses to her.)

MR. BINGLEY

Miss Bennet; what a pleasant surprise.

ELIZABETH

Good morning. I was most anxious to receive Jane's note and hear of her illness and am come to check on her.

MISS BINGLEY

Your hem, my dear Miss Elizabeth! Did your carriage get stuck in the mud?

ELIZABETH

(Looks down at her hemline.)
No, it did not, for I walked.

MRS. HURST

Walked! All the way from Longbourn, in this weather!

ELIZABETH

It is a mere three miles and the rain stopped before breakfast.
(Notices that **MR. DARCY** is looking at her and turns back to **MR. BINGLEY**.)
I was most concerned about my sister.

MR. BINGLEY

Of course you were. I am sure she will feel much the better
now you are here. Mr. Jones feels that several days of bed rest
will do her much good. I would be most happy to send to
Longbourn for your things, so you can care for your sister.

ELIZABETH

I never meant to imply...

MR. BINGLEY

I assure you, it will be no problem at all.

ELIZABETH

You are too kind, Sir. Now, if would you be so good as to take
me to my sister?

MR. BINGLEY

Yes, yes, of course. Right this way.

> (Gestures for the **FOOTMAN** to show her.
> They exit.)

MR. HURST

Here now, if I must be awake, let us at least make up a table
of quadrille.

> (**MR. BINGLEY**, **MISS BINGLEY**, and
> **MRS. HURST** cross to the table where they
> sit and begin to play cards.)

MRS. HURST

I must say, Miss Elizabeth Bennet has nothing to recommend
her, but being an excellent walker. Did you note her
appearance? She looked almost wild.

MISS BINGLEY

She did indeed, Louisa. I could hardly keep my countenance.
Why must she be scampering about the country, because her

sister had a cold? Her hair so untidy, so blowzy.

MRS. HURST

And her petticoats. Six inches deep in mud.

MR. BINGLEY

It quite escaped my notice. I thought she looked remarkable well.

MISS BINGLEY

I'm sure you noticed it, Mr. Darcy. I'm inclined to think that you would not wish to see your sister make such an exhibition.

MR. DARCY

Certainly not.

MRS. HURST

To walk three or four miles, in all that dirt, and quite alone!

MISS BINGLEY

It shows an abominable sort of conceited independence.

MR. BINGLEY

It shows an affection for her sister that is very pleasing.

MISS BINGLEY

I'm afraid, Mr. Darcy, that this adventure has affected your admiration for her fine eyes?

MR. DARCY

Not at all. I thought they were brightened by the exercise.
    (This surprised both women and caused a
    pause in the conversation.)

MRS. HURST
Well, Jane Bennet is a sweet girl. But with such a father and mother.

MISS BINGLEY
She told us that their uncle is an attorney in Meryton.

MRS. HURST
And another who lives in Cheapside.
                    (Both women laugh.)

MR. BINGLEY
If they had uncles enough to fill all Cheapside, it would not make them one jot less agreeable.

DARCY
But it must lessen their chance of marrying well.

                    (**ELIZABETH** enters. They all stand and
                    bow/curtsey.)

MISS BINGLEY
And how did you find your dear sister?

ELIZABETH
I am afraid that she is still feeling poorly.

MR. BINGLEY
Let me send for Mr. Jones.

ELIZABETH
Let us see how she fares come morning.

MRS. HURST
Would you join us for a hand of cards, Miss Bennet?

ELIZABETH

Thank you, no. I want to check on Jane in a while and will just amuse myself with a book.
>   (She picks up a book and sits down.)

MR. HURST

You prefer reading to cards? Singular.

MISS BINGLEY

Miss Elizabeth Bennet despises card and is a great reader and has no pleasure in anything else.

ELIZABETH

I deserve neither such praise or such censure. I am not a great reader and find pleasure in many things.

MISS BINGLEY

And you sir, Mr. Darcy, what pray are you doing?

MR. DARCY

I am writing to my sister, Georgiana.

MISS BINGLEY

Ah, Georgiana! Is she much grown since last spring? Will she be as tall as I am?

MR. DARCY

I would think that she is now about Miss Elizabeth Bennet's height.

MISS BINGLEY

How I long to see her again. Such a countenance, such manners, and so accomplished for her age. Her performance on the pianoforte is exquisite.

MR. BINGLEY

It is amazing to me how young ladies are so very

accomplished. They paint screens, they speak French, they dance, they play the pianoforte and I know not what.

MR. DARCY

I cannot boast of knowing more than half a dozen in the whole range of my acquaintance that are truly accomplished.

ELIZABETH

You must comprehend a great deal in your idea of an accomplished woman.

MR. DARCY

I do.

MISS BINGLEY

To be esteemed truly accomplished, a woman must have a thorough knowledge of music, singing, drawing, dancing and the modern languages. And besides this, must possess a certain something in her air and address, and her expression.

MR. DARCY

And to all this she must yet add the improvement of her mind through extensive reading.

ELIZABETH

I am surprised at your knowing six such women.

MISS BINGLEY

You are too severe on your sex, Miss Bennet. Louisa and I know many such women who answer this description.

MRS. HURST

Caroline is correct. We know many accomplished ladies. Why there's...

MR. HURST

Here, here, are we going to talk or play cards?

(They return to their card playing and
ELIZABETH opens her book. **MR. DARCY**
waits a moment and then – when everyone is
busy - turns to watch **ELIZABETH**.)

(BLACKOUT)

ACT I

Scene 5

SETTING: The Bennet parlor.

AT RISE: The Bennet family are all present.

MR. BENNET
Well, Jane, Elizabeth I am glad you are come home.

JANE
Thank you, Father. I am glad to be home.

ELIZABETH
Indeed.

MRS. BENNET
I do wish you had stayed at Netherfield longer. One can never be too cautious.

MR. BENNET
Cautious over her health, my dear or cautious over Mr. Bingley's attentions?

MRS. BENNET
Why, over...
                    (Realizes he is teasing her. Half laugh.)
Oh Mr. Bennet, you do delight in teasing me.

                    (They all laugh.)

MR. BENNET
I hope, my dear, that you have ordered a good dinner today, because I have reason to expect an addition to our family party.

(Takes out his pocket watch and looks at it.)
In fact, I expect him momentarily.

MRS. BENNET
Who do you mean, my dear?

MR. BENNET
The gentleman is a person whom I have never saw in the
whole of my life. About a month ago, I received this letter
(Takes a letter from his coat pocket.)
and as I thought it was a case requiring some delicacy,
answered about a fortnight ago. It is from my cousin, Mr.
Collins, who, when I am dead, may turn you all out of this
house as soon as he pleases.

MRS. BENNET
Pray do not talk of that odious man. I do think it is the
hardest thing in the world, that your estate should be
entailed away from your own children.

MR. BENNET
Nothing can clear Mr. Collins from the guilt of inheriting
Longbourn. But, if you will listen to his letter, you may be
softened by his intentions.
(Reads.)
Dear Sir, The disagreement subsisting between yourself and
my late honored father always gave me much uneasiness.
Since I have had the misfortune to lose him, I have frequently
wished to heal the breach. Having received ordination at
Easter, I have been so fortunate as to be distinguished by the
patronage of the Right Honorable Lady Catherine DeBourgh,
whose beneficence has awarded me the rectory of the parish.
As a clergyman, I feel it my duty to promote the blessings of
peace in all the families within my reach. I am concerned with
the circumstances of my inheriting Longbourn and wish to
assure you of my desire to make amends to your girls. If you
have no objection, I propose myself of the satisfaction of

waiting on you and your family on Monday the 18th and shall probably trespass on your hospitality till the following Saturday.'

MRS. BENNET

Well, if he is disposed to make amends to our girls, I shall not discourage him.

ELIZABETH

What do you think, Father; can he be a sensible man?

MR. BENNET

No, my dear, I think not. In fact, I have great hopes of finding him quite the reverse.

          (Door bell sounds.)

Well, Mr. Collins appears to be a punctual young man, I'll give him that.

(HILL enters.)

HILL

Mr. Collins.

(MR. COLLINS enters and crosses to **MR.** and **MRS. BENNET.)**

MR. COLLINS

          (Bows to each.)

My dear Mr. Bennet. Mrs. Bennet.

MR. BENNET

          (Bows.)

Mr. Collins.

MRS. BENNET

          (Curtsies.)

My dear Mr. Collins, you are most welcome to Longbourn.
These are our daughters, Jane, Elizabeth, Mary, Kitty, and
Lydia.

(They curtsey.)

MR. COLLINS

Ah, my fair cousins. My dear Mr. Bennet, Mrs. Bennet, I must
compliment you on your daughters. I had heard much of their
beauty, but fame had fallen short of the truth. I have no doubt
of your seeing them disposed of in blessed bonds of marriage
in due time.
(Looks at **JANE** again and smiles.)
I have no doubt at all.

MRS. BENNET

You are very kind, sir, I am sure, and I wish with all my heart
that you may be proved correct. Won't you sit down?
(She pours a cup of tea for him.)

MR. COLLINS

I must say, Ma'am, that I have rarely had the pleasure to sit
down in such fine company. Save, of course, for the evenings I
have dined at Rosings Park. For I assure you that Lady
Catherine DeBourgh sets the most elegant table imaginable.

MR. BENNET

You seem to be most fortunate in your patroness, sir.

MR. COLLINS

Yes, indeed. I have never in my life witnessed such behavior
in a person of rank – such affability and condescension – as I
have experienced from Lady Catherine. She has asked me
twice to dine at Rosings, and had even sent for me to make up
a fourth at quadrille. She once paid a visit to my humble
parsonage, where she approved some alterations I had
undertaken and even suggested the placement of shelves in

the closets up stairs.

MR. BENNET
Indeed? She seems most concerned with your personal welfare.

MR. COLLINS
She is indeed. She has even condescended to advise me to marry as soon as I can, provided I choose with discretion. Which indeed I shall. A young woman of gentle birth and quiet ways I'm sure would please Lady Catherine...ah, I mean, myself.
(He looks at **JANE** and smiles.)

MRS. BENNET
Does she live near you, sir?

MR. COLLINS
The garden in which stands my humble abode is separated only by a lane from Rosings Park.

MRS. BENNET
I think you said she was a widow, sir. Has she any family?

MR. COLLINS
She has only one daughter, the heiress of Rosings and of very extensive property.

MRS. BENNET
Has Miss DeBourgh been presented at court?

MR. COLLINS
She is unfortunately of a sickly constitution, preventing her from being presented which, as I told Lady Catherine myself, deprived the British court of its brightest ornament... You may imagine that I am happy on every occasion to offer those little delicate compliments which are always acceptable to

ladies.

MR. BENNET
It is happy that you possess the talent for flattering with delicacy. May I ask, sir, whether these pleasing attentions proceed from the impulse of the moment, or are the result of previous study?

MR. COLLINS
They arise chiefly from what is passing at the time and, although I sometimes amuse myself with arranging such little elegant compliments as may be adapted to the ordinary situation, I always wish to give them as unstudied an air as possible.

MR. BENNET
Indeed?
> (He gets up to refresh his tea.)

MR. COLLINS
> (Looks around the room.)

I compliment you, Madame, on a most comfortable room. It takes the delicate female touch to turn a house into a home. I'm sure it will not be long before my fair cousins will be mistresses of their own homes.
> (Looks at **JANE** and smiles.)

MRS. BENNET
> (Understands his meaning, lowers her voice.)

Well, sir, as to my younger daughters, I cannot positively answer, but I feel it is incumbent on me to hint that Jane will likely to be very soon engaged.

MR. COLLINS
Ah...I understand, ma'am.
> (Looks at **ELIZABETH** and smiles.)

ELIZABETH
Mother, perhaps Mr. Collins would care to see your garden.

MRS. BENNET
Do you care for gardening, Sir?

MR. COLLINS
Indeed I do, ma'am. When my duties permits me leisure, I enjoy tending to growing things.
> (They begin to exit and he continues talking.
> **MR. BENNET** exits the other way.)

I confess I have received a number of compliments on my gardens as being the most beautiful in the area...with the exception, of course, of the gardens at Rosings....

> (Door bell sounds. **HILL** enters followed by **DENNY** and **WICKHAM**.)

HILL
Mr. Denny and Mr. Wickham.

LYDIA
Denny!
> (She and **KITTY** cross to the men.)

You're back! We had hoped you were.

DENNY
Ladies. I returned this morning and came as soon as I could to call. May I introduce my friend, Mr. Wickham, who has just accepted a commission in the corps?

> (Bows and curtsies. **HILL** enters again, with **MR. BINGLEY** and **MR. DARCY**.)

HILL
Mr. Bingley and Mr. Darcy.
> (Bows/curtsies.)

MR. BINGLEY

Good afternoon, ladies. Darcy and I came to Longbourn on purpose to enquire after Miss Bennet's health.

JANE

How kind you are, sir. I am much better.
>   (Bows.)
And I believe you know Mr. Denny?
>   (Bows.)
And this is Mr. Wickham, who has just joined the militia in Meryton.

>   (**MR. DARCY** and **MR. WICKHAM** are
>   startled to see each other. After a few
>   moments, **MR. WICKHAM** touches his hat
>   and **MR. DARCY** coldly turns away. Only
>   **ELIZABETH** notices. This all goes on during
>   the conversation.)

MR. BINGLEY

I also came to deliver an invitation to Netherfield next week for our ball.

>   (He hands the invitation to **JANE**. General
>   excitement from the girls over a ball.)
And Miss Bennet, would you do me the honor of saving the first dance for me?

JANE

I would be most delighted, sir.

ELIZABETH

Would you take a cup of tea, sir?

MR. BINGLEY

Sadly we cannot. For I promised Caroline and Louisa to see that all the invitations were delivered today. In fact, we must leave now. Please convey our regards to your parents. Until next week. Ladies.

> (Curtsies and bows.)

Gentlemen.

> (Bows. **MR. BINGLEY** and **MR. DARCY**
> exit. **MRS. BENNET** and **MR. COLLINS**
> enter.)

MRS. BENNET
Was that Mr. Bingley and Mr. Darcy we just saw leaving?

JANE
It was...

LYDIA
> (Interrupts **JANE,** crosses to her and takes
> the invitation from her and hands it to her
> mother.)

They came to deliver an invitation to the ball at Netherfield.

> (**MRS. BENNET** opens the invitation.)

MRS. BENNET
What an elegant invitation.

MARY
As long as I can have the morning to myself for study, I shall
have no disinclination for it. I think it is no sacrifice to join
occasionally in evening engagements.

MRS. BENNET
Mr. Bingley has extended the invitation to any guests who
may be visiting. Would you care to join us, Mr. Collins?

MR. COLLINS
I would indeed. How beneficent of Mr. Bingley.

ELIZABETH
Do you think it proper to join in the evening's amusement?

MR. COLLINS
You concern does you justice, my dear cousin. But I assure
you that a ball of this kind, given by a young man of
character, to respectable people, can have no evil tendency. So
far from objecting, I shall hope to be honored with the hands
of all my fair cousins in the course of the evening; and I take
this opportunity to soliciting yours, Cousin Elizabeth, for the
first two dances.

ELIZABETH
Oh...ah....
> (Can't figure a way out.)

I thank you, sir.
> (**ELIZABETH** moves away from **MR.
> COLLINS** and crosses to sit behind the tea
> table.)

LYDIA
Will you and the other officers go to the Netherfield Ball,
Denny?

DENNY
Mr. Darcy spoke to Col Forester about the ball and it was
announced that as many of us as can be excused from our
duties may attend.

> (**MR. WICKHAM** crosses to **ELIZABETH**.)

WICKHAM
How far is Netherfield from Meryton?

ELIZABETH
No more than three miles.

WICKHAM

How long has Mr. Darcy been staying there?

ELIZABETH

About a month. He is a man of very large property in Derbyshire, I understand.

WICKHAM

Yes, his estate there is a noble one. I have been connected with his family from infancy. My father was the late Mr. Darcy's steward.
                    (**ELIZABETH** appears shocked.)
You may well be surprised, Miss Bennet, after seeing - as you probably did - the very cold manner of our meeting. Are you much acquainted with Mr. Darcy?

ELIZABETH

As much as I ever wish to be. He is not at all liked in Hertfordshire.

WICKHAM

I cannot pretend to be sorry. His father, Miss Bennet, was one of the best men that ever breathed. He was my godfather and was excessively attached to me. Knowing that it was my wish to go into the church, the late Mr. Darcy bequeathed the living to me when it next came available. However, after his father's death, when the living came, the present Mr. Darcy gave it elsewhere.

ELIZABETH

Good heavens! This is quite shocking! He deserves to be publicly disgraced.

WICKHAM

Some time or other he will be – but it shall not be by me. 'Til I can forget his father, I can never defy or expose him.

ELIZABETH

But what can have been his motive to behave so cruelly?

WICKHAM

A dislike of me, which I cannot but attribute to some measure of jealousy. Had the late Mr. Darcy liked me less, his son might have borne me better.

ELIZABETH

I had not thought Mr. Darcy so bad as this, though I have never liked him.

WICKHAM

All his actions may be traced to pride, for pride has often been his best friend.

ELIZABETH

Has such abominable pride as his ever done him good?

WICKHAM

Yes, it has often led him to be generous, to display hospitality, to assist his tenants, and relieve the poor. He has also brotherly pride, and affection, which makes him a kind and careful guardian of his sister.

ELIZABETH

What sort of a girl is Miss Darcy?

WICKHAM

As a child, she was affectionate and pleasing, and extremely fond of me. She is a pretty girl, about sixteen – about the age of your sister Lydia.

ELIZABETH

Lydia is but fifteen. I am astonished at Mr. Darcy's intimacy with Mr. Bingley. How can Mr. Bingley, who is truly amiable, be in friendship with such a man? He cannot know what Mr.

Darcy is.

WICKHAM
Probably not. Mr. Darcy can please where he chooses. Among those who are his equals in consequence, he is a very different man.

> (They overhear **MR. COLLINS** for a moment.)

MR. COLLINS
...and the chimney piece alone in one of Lady Catherine DeBourgh's drawing rooms cost eight hundred pounds...

WICKHAM
Is your cousin intimately acquainted with Lady Catherine DeBourgh?

ELIZABETH
Lady Catherine has very lately given him a living and I do not think she could have found a more grateful recipient.

WICKHAM
Perhaps you do not know, but Lady Catherine is Mr. Darcy's aunt. Her daughter, Miss DeBourgh, will have a very large fortune. It is believed that she and Mr. Darcy will unite the two estates.

ELIZABETH
Indeed? From what I understand of Miss DeBourgh, I think she will suit him quite nicely.

(BLACKOUT)

ACT I

Scene 6

SETTING: Netherfield ballroom.

AT RISE: The Bennets enter and are greeted by
MR. BINGLEY and **MISS BINGLEY. MR.** and
MRS. BENNET and **MARY** cross to some chairs near
SIR WILLIAM. LYDIA and **KITTY** cross to **MARIA
LUCAS. JANE** and **ELIZABETH** cross to
CHARLOTTE LUCAS. MR. DARCY is talking to
MR. and **MRS. HURST.**

ELIZABETH
Charlotte. It's so good to see you.

CHARLOTTE
It's good to see you Elizabeth. And you Jane. It appears that
everyone in Hertfordshire is here tonight.

                    (**MR. BINGLEY** crosses to **MR.** and **MRS.**
                    BENNET.)

MRS. BENNET
                    (Calls out.)
Jane? Jane!

JANE
It appears our mother needs me. If you will excuse me.
                    (**JANE** crosses to her mother who obviously
                    wanted her to talk with **MR. BINGLEY.**)

CHARLOTTE
Jane looks quite happy since Mr. Bingley has been in the
neighborhood and it would appear that he greatly admires
her.

ELIZABETH

Yes, it does. If he should fall in love with her and the feelings are returned, I would be quite happy for her.

CHARLOTTE

She should show more affection, in order to secure him.

ELIZABETH

Secure him?

CHARLOTTE

Yes. Jane should make the most of every opportunity to command his attention.

ELIZABETH

But she is not certain yet of her regard for him. She has not known him long enough to understand his character or know whether they would be happy in marriage.

CHARLOTTE

Happiness in marriage is entirely a matter of chance. It is better to know as little as possible of the defects of the person with whom you are to pass your life.

(**LYDIA** and **KITTY** bring **DENNY** over to **ELIZABETH**. Bow/curtsies.)

DENNY

Good evening Ladies.

ELIZABETH

Good evening, Mr. Denny.

LYDIA

Lizzy, what do you think? Wickham is not here!

ELIZABETH

Oh?

DENNY

No. As I told your sisters, he was obliged to go to town on business.

(Pause, aside to **ELIZABETH**.)

I do not imagine his business would have called him away just now, if he had not wished to avoid a certain gentleman.

ELIZABETH

I understand.

KITTY

Come, Denny, it's nearly time for dancing and we have to find another gentleman.

(He smiles, shrugs, bows and lets **KITTY** and **LYDIA** pull him away. **MR. COLLINS** crosses to them.)

MR. COLLINS

Cousin Elizabeth.

ELIZABETH

Charlotte Lucas, may I present our cousin, Mr. Collins?

(They bow/curtsey as the music starts. He smiles at **ELIZABETH**.)

MR. COLLINS

Cousin Elizabeth?

(**ELIZABETH** smiles at **CHARLOTTE**, and moves into the dance with him. He is a clumsy dancer, and apologizes profusely each time he makes a mistake. **ELIZABETH** is mortified and relieved when the dance is over

and she returns to **CHARLOTTE**. She is
quite surprised when **MR. DARCY** crosses.)

MR. DARCY
(Bows.)
Miss Lucas, Miss Bennet.

ELIZABETH/CHARLOTTE
(Curtsies.)
Mr. Darcy.

MR. DARCY
Miss Bennet, may I have the honor of your hand for the next
dance?

ELIZABETH
I...I...I thank you, sir, yes.

(**MR. DARCY** extends his arm; **ELIZABETH**
takes it. They begin dancing and for a moment
are silent. Their conversation goes throughout
the movements of the dance.)

ELIZABETH
Are we to go through the entire dance without speaking, sir? I
could comment on the fact that this is one of the more
common dances and you could make some kind of remark
about the size of the room or the number of the couples.

MR. DARCY
Do you talk by rule, then, while you are dancing?

ELIZABETH
One must speak a little, you know; and yet, for the advantage
of some, conversation ought to be so arranged, that they may
have the trouble of saying as little as possible.

MR. DARCY

Does Mr. Denny often visit Longbourn?

ELIZABETH

Yes. When you came the other day, he had just introduced us to a new acquaintance.

MR. DARCY

Mr. Wickham is blessed with such happy manners as may ensure his making friends – whether he may be equally capable of retaining them, is less certain.

ELIZABETH

He has been so unlucky as to lose your friendship and in a manner which he is likely to suffer from all his life... I remember hearing you once say that you hardly ever forgave, and that your resentment - once created - was unappeasable.

MR. DARCY

I did. May I ask to what these questions tend?

ELIZABETH

Merely to the illustration of your character. I am trying to make it out.

MR. DARCY

And what is your success?

ELIZABETH

I do not get on at all. I hear such different accounts of you as to puzzle me exceedingly.

MR. DARCY

I can readily believe that. I could wish, Miss Bennet, that you were not to sketch my character at the present moment.

ELIZABETH
But if I do not take your likeness now, I may never have
another opportunity.

MR. DARCY
I would by no means suspend any pleasure of yours.

(**SIR WILLIAM** interrupts.)

SIR WILLIAM
My dear Mr. Darcy, I have been most gratified indeed. Such
superior dancing is not often seen. I must hope to have this
pleasure often repeated, when a certain desirable event takes
place, eh, Miss Elizabeth?
        (Glances at **MR. BINGLEY** and **JANE**.)
What congratulations will then flow in.

        (The music ends. **MR. DARCY** takes her
        back, bows, and leaves. A moment later, **MISS
        BINGLEY** crosses to her.)

MISS BINGLEY
So, Miss Elizabeth, I hear you are delighted with George
Wickham. I am sure that the young man forgot to tell you,
among his other communications, that he was the son of the
late Mr. Darcy's steward. Let me recommend you, however, as
a friend, not to give confidence to all his assertions. Wickham
has treated Mr. Darcy in a most infamous manner.

ELIZABETH
His guilt and his descent appear by your account to be the
same. For I have heard you accuse him of nothing worse than
being the son of Mr. Darcy's steward, which I assure you, he
informed me himself.

MISS BINGLEY
I beg your pardon. Excuse my interference; it was kindly

meant.

(MISS BINGLEY crosses to her sister.
ELIZABETH crosses to **JANE**, fuming.)

ELIZABETH
Insolent girl! To try to denigrate Mr. Wickham in defense of
Mr. Darcy.

JANE
Elizabeth, it may be there is more to the story than we know.
For, although Mr. Bingley does not know the whole, he is
certain Mr. Wickham is by no means a respectable young
man.

ELIZABETH
Mr. Bingley does not know Mr. Wickham himself?

JANE
No, not at all.

ELIZABETH
This account then, is what he received from Mr. Darcy. Mr.
Bingley's defense is a very able one, but I shall venture still to
think of both gentlemen as I did before.

JANE
Elizabeth, look.

(MR. COLLINS crosses to **MR. DARCY.)**

ELIZABETH
What can he mean? They have not been properly introduced.
To speak to Mr. Darcy would be the height of impropriety.

MR. COLLINS
My dear sir, I have just found out that you are the nephew of

my noble patroness, Lady Catherine DeBourgh. It is my
pleasure to be able to inform you, sir, that her ladyship was in
excellent health when last I saw her, a week ago.

MR. DARCY
(Stands. Coldly.)
And what is your name, sir?

MR. COLLINS
Collins, sir.

(**MR. DARCY** walks away. **MR. COLLINS**
does not notice the snub, but bows instead.
ELIZABETH and **JANE** are mortified. There
is a lull in the music. **MRS. BENNET**, who is
talking loudly enough to be clearly heard.)

MRS. BENNET
And we are daily expecting to announce Jane's engagement to
Mr. Bingley. Which will be a good thing for the other girls, for
that will throw them in that way of other rich men.

MR. BINGLEY
(To cover the embarrassment.)
Perhaps we should have some music?

(**MRS. HURST** stands, but **MARY** rushes offstage. A moment later, piano music is heard
and **MARY** begins to sing poorly. **LYDIA** and
KITTY run through the room, with **DENNY'S**
sword. **DENNY** chases them. **ELIZABETH**
and **JANE** look at each other in shocked
embarrassment.)

(BLACKOUT)

ACT I

Scene 7

SETTING: The Bennet parlor.

AT RISE: **ELIZABETH** and **KITTY** are arranging flowers in a vase. **MRS. BENNET** enters with **MR. COLLINS**.

MRS. BENNET
Elizabeth, Mr. Collins has something he wishes to say to you. Kitty, I need you upstairs.

ELIZABETH
Please, ma'am. Do not go. Mr. Collins can have nothing to say to me that anybody need not hear.

MRS. BENNET
Nonsense! I *insist* upon your staying and hearing Mr. Collins. Come Kitty.

(They exit. **ELIZABETH** sits.)

MR. COLLINS
My dear Cousin Elizabeth, you can hardly doubt the purpose of my discourse; your modesty, so far from doing you any disservice, adds to your other perfections. You must know that, almost as soon as I entered this house, I singled you out as the companion of my future life. But perhaps it would be advisable for me to state my reasons for marrying.

First, I think it a right thing for every clergyman to set the example of matrimony in his parish. Secondly, I am convinced that it will add greatly to my happiness. And thirdly – which perhaps I ought to have mentioned earlier – that is it the particular recommendation of my noble patroness. "Mr.

Collins," said she, "you must marry. Choose properly. Choose
a gentlewoman for *my* sake and for your own. Let her be an
active useful sort of person. Find such a woman, bring her to
Hunsford, and *I* will visit her."

I assure you, there are many amiable young women in my
parish. But the fact that I am to inherit this estate after the
death of your honored father, I could not satisfy myself
without choosing a wife from among his daughters.

Now, nothing remains for me but to assure you in the most
animated language of the violence of my affections. I will
make no demands upon your father and you may be assured
that no reproach on your lack of dowry will ever pass my lips
once we are married.

ELIZABETH
You are too hasty, sir. You forget I have not given you my
answer. Let me do it without further loss of time. I thank you
for the compliment. I am sensible of the honor of your
proposal, but it is impossible for me to do otherwise than
decline.

MR. COLLINS
I understand that is it usual with young ladies to reject the
addresses of the man whom they secretly mean to accept. I
am, therefore, by no means discouraged and hope to lead you
to the altar ere long.

ELIZABETH
I assure you, sir, that I am not one of those young ladies. I am
perfectly serious. You could not make me happy and I am
convinced that I am the last woman in the world who could
make you happy.

MR. COLLINS
I realize that my station in life, my connections with the noble

family of DeBourgh, are circumstances highly in my favor. In spite of your manifold attractions, it is by no means certain that you will ever receive another offer of marriage and I must assume that it is your wish of increasing love by suspense, which is the usual practice of elegant females.

ELIZABETH

I do assure you, sir, that I have no pretentions to that kind of elegance which consists of tormenting a respectable man. I thank you again for the honor you have done me, but to accept them is absolutely impossible.

MR. COLLINS

You are uniformly charming and I am persuaded that, when sanctioned by both your excellent parents, my proposal will not fail. In fact, your mother was so pleased with my situation that she has gone to call your father here.

> (**ELIZABETH** is so frustrated that she cannot speak and sits. A moment later, **MRS. BENNET** enters. **MRS. BENNET** senses that something is not right and crosses to **MR. COLLINS** to have a quiet conversation, which grows in animation. After a moment, it is obvious that she has instructed him to leave everything to her. **MR. COLLINS** exits. After a frustrated look at **ELIZABETH**, **MRS. BENNET** opens the door to the parlor to find **MR. BENNET** standing there.)

MRS. BENNET

Mr. Bennet, you are wanted immediately. You must come and make Lizzy marry Mr. Collins. For she vows she will not have him and, if you do not make haste, he will change his mind and not have her.

MR. BENNET
I have not the pleasure of understanding you. Of what are you talking?

MRS. BENNET
Of Mr. Collins and Lizzy. Lizzy declares she will not have Mr. Collins and Mr. Collins begins to say that he will not have Lizzy.

MR. BENNET
And what am I to do on the occasion? It seems a hopeless business.

MRS. BENNET
Speak to Lizzy yourself. Tell her that you insist upon her marrying him.

MR. BENNET
Lizzy? Come here, child.
          (**ELIZABETH** crosses to her father.)
I understand that Mr. Collins has made you an offer of marriage. Is that true?

ELIZABETH
Yes, sir.

MR. BENNET
Very well; and you have refused this offer of marriage?

ELIZABETH
I have, sir.

MR. BENNET
Very well. We now come to the point. Your mother insists upon your accepting it. Is it not so, Mrs. Bennet?

MRS. BENNET

Yes, or I will never see her again.

MR. BENNET

An unhappy alternative is before you, Elizabeth. From this day you must be a stranger to one of your parents. Your mother will never see you again if you do *not* marry Mr. Collins ... and I will never see you again if you *do*.

(**ELIZABETH** smiles, obviously relieved.)

MRS. BENNET
(Whines.)

Oh, Mr. Bennet!

(BLACKOUT)

ACT I

Scene 8

SETTING: The Bennet parlor.

AT RISE: The whole Bennet family is present
except for **LYDIA** and **KITTY**.

MR. BENNET
I must say that it was most kind of the Lucases to invite Mr.
Collins to dine with them this evening.

MRS. BENNET
Oh, do not speak of him, Mr. Bennet. I tell you what, Miss
Lizzy, if you take it into your head to go on refusing every
offer of marriage in this way, you will never get a husband at
all – and I do not know who is to maintain you when your
father is dead.

(**LYDIA** and **KITTY** enter in a rush.)

MRS. BENNET
My goodness. Whatever is the matter?

KITTY
We just came from Meryton, and you'll never guess.

LYDIA
Mr. Collins has offered a proposal of marriage to Charlotte
Lucas -

KITTY
(Finishes her sentence.)
- and she has accepted him.

MRS. BENNET

What!

(Looks at **ELIZABETH** who is not surprised.)
You do not seemed surprised to hear this news, Lizzy.

ELIZABETH

I am not, ma'am, for Charlotte told me of it when I called this
morning. He had just asked her and she asked me to keep it
private until her parents had spoken to Mr. Collins.

KITTY

To think of Charlotte and Mr. Collins married.

ELIZABETH

I admit I too was surprised when I first learned that
Charlotte had accepted Mr. Collins' proposal of marriage. But
then she explained her reasons to me.

JANE

What did she say?

ELIZABETH

She said, "Do you think it incredible that Mr. Collins should
be able to procure any woman's good opinion, because he was
not so happy as to succeed with you?"

MARY

That is a good thought.

ELIZABETH

Charlotte is not romantic, you know. She never was. She asks
only a comfortable home; and, considering Mr. Collin's
character, connections, and situation in life, she is convinced
that her chance of happiness with him is as fair as most
people can boast on entering the marriage state.

JANE

That is how many people think on marriage.

ELIZABETH

Undoubtedly, but how sad to marry someone for whom you have no affection, no respect.

MRS. BENNET

So, Lizzy, I have no doubt that Charlotte Lucas is counting the days until she is mistress of Longbourn.

ELIZABETH

I do not think she would talk of that to me, ma'am.

MRS. BENNET

And now Mr. Bingley has left; when we had such hopes of him.

ELIZABETH

What?

(Looks at **JANE**.)

I thought Mr. Bingley was going to town for a few days to attend to business.

JANE

I had a letter this morning from Caroline Bingley. She said that Mr. Bingley imagined that his business could not be concluded in three or four days. So the whole party has left Netherfield and are on their way back to town and have no intention to come back again.

She goes on to state that Mr. Darcy is impatient to see his sister, as she is herself, in the hopes that one day soon, she will be able to address Miss Darcy as 'sister.' It is obvious that Mr. Bingley has long cared for Miss Darcy and – suspecting how I felt about her brother – Miss Bingley most kindly meant to put me on my guard.

MRS. BENNET

And now Mr. Bingley is gone for good. Ah, well...Come girls, it's near supper. Lydia, Kitty would you please go call your father? He is reading in the garden. Mary, come with me...

(**MRS. BENNETT** and **MARY** exit.)

ELIZABETH

Oh, Jane...

JANE

I will not repine. He will be forgotten and we shall all be as we were before. He may live in my memory as the most amiable man of my acquaintance, but that is all. I have this comfort, that it has not been more than a fancy on my part and it has done no harm to anyone but myself.

ELIZABETH

My dear Jane, you are too good. Your sweetness and disinterestedness are really angelic. I feel as if I had never done you justice or loved you as you deserve.

(They hug and **JANE** exits. **MR. BENNET** enters with a book in his hand.)

ELIZABETH

Reading in the garden?

MR. BENNET

I had hoped to escape the turmoil in the house. An hour does not pass without your mother lamenting the loss of two potential marriages in the family.

ELIZABETH

Father...

MR. BENNET

I know, my dear. I would not have you married to someone as
unworthy of you as Mr. Collins. But Jane... So, Lizzy, your
sister is crossed in love. I congratulate her. Next to being
married, a girl likes to be crossed in love a little now and
then. It gives her a distinction among her companions. When
is your time to come? You will hardly bear to be long outdone
by Jane. Let Wickham be your man. He is a pleasant fellow
and would jilt you creditably.

ELIZABETH

Thank you, sir, but a less agreeable man would satisfy me.
We must not all expect Jane's good fortune.

MR. BENNET

True, but it is a comfort to think that, whatever of that kind
may befall you, you have an affectionate mother who will
always make the most of it.

> (**MR. BENNET** exits. Lights fade.)

> (Lights up on the Bennet parlor, where a
> small party is being given. In addition to the
> Bennet family, **MR.** and **MRS. GARDINER**
> are present, along with **DENNY**, **WICKHAM**,
> and **CHARLOTTE**. **MRS. BENNET** and
> **MRS. GARDINER** are seated, talking.)

MRS. BENNET

It is the grievous thing, sister, to think that two of my girls
were on the point of marriage and now nothing has come of it.
I do not blame Jane, for she would have got Mr. Bingley is she
could. But Lizzy! Oh sister! It is very hard to think that she
might have been Mr. Collins wife by this time. Now Lady
Lucas will have a daughter married before I have and
Charlotte will become mistress of Longbourn. The Lucases
are very artful people indeed. They are all for what they can

get. I am sorry to say it of them, but so it is. However, we are glad that you and my brother have come to us and to hear what you tell us of long sleeves.

(**ELIZABETH** crosses to the ladies with **WICKHAM**.)

ELIZABETH
I would like to present Mr. Wickham to you, Aunt. This is my Aunt Gardiner, who is married to my mother's brother.

WICKHAM
(Bows.)
A pleasure to meet you ma'am. Miss Bennet tells me that you are familiar with Derbyshire.

MRS. GARDINER
Yes, indeed, sir. I spent many happy years in Derbyshire and believe it to be the most beautiful in all of England.

WICKHAM
I must agree with you, ma'am. Are you familiar with Pemberley? I only ask because I grew up there.

MRS. GARDINER
I have heard of it, but never had the opportunity to see it.

(**KITTY** and **LYDIA** come up with **DENNY**.)

LYDIA
Come, Wickham, Mary is going to play some music for us to dance.

(He bows to the ladies and **KITTY**, **LYDIA**, **WICKHAM**, **DENNY**, and **MARY** exit. A moment later, music is heard. **MRS. BENNET** snubs **ELIZABETH** and gets up,

with an ad lib about checking on the
refreshments, and crosses the room.
ELIZABETH sits next to **MRS.
GARDINER**.)

MRS. GARDINER
Your mother has been talking to me of Jane and Mr. Bingley.

ELIZABETH
Poor Jane! I am sorry for her. She says otherwise but, with
her disposition, she may not get over it immediately.

MRS. GARDINER
Do you think she would be prevailed on to go back to London
with her Uncle Gardiner and me? A change of scene may be
as useful as anything.

ELIZABETH
What a wonderful offer. I am sure that Jane will readily
accept.

MRS. GARDINER
She need not fear a chance meeting with Mr. Bingley. We live
in so different a part of town; it is improbable they should
meet at all, unless he comes to see her.

ELIZABETH
That is quite impossible, for he is in the custody of his friend
and Mr. Darcy would not suffer Mr. Bingley to call on Jane.

MRS. GARDINER
Then I shall go immediately and ask Jane.

(She crosses to **JANE** while **CHARLOTTE**
crosses to **ELIZABETH** and sits.)

CHARLOTTE
Eliza, I shall depend on hearing from you often.

ELIZABETH
Then you certainly shall.

CHARLOTTE
I am not likely to leave Kent for some time. Promise me you will come to Hunsford. My father and Maria are to come in March and I hope you will consent to be part of their party. Indeed you will be as welcome as either of them.

ELIZABETH
I will most certainly come, Charlotte, if nothing more than to see the famed fireplace at Rosings.
(They both laugh.)

(BLACKOUT)

ACT I

Scene 9

SETTING: The Collins' parlor.

AT RISE: **CHARLOTTE** and **MR. COLLINS**,
SIR WILLIAM, **MARIA**, and **ELIZABETH** enter.

MR. COLLINS

And from our parlor you can see, Sir William, if you but look
out this window and beyond those trees, is Rosings Park. We
are not but a few steps away when Lady Catherine invites us
to dine and are never allowed to walk home. Her Ladyship's
carriage is called for us; *one* of Her Ladyship's carriages, for
she has several.

SIR WILLIAM
(Looking out the window.)

I see.

CHARLOTTE

Lady Catherine is a most attentive neighbor.

MR. COLLINS

Very true, my dear. She is the sort of woman whom one
cannot regard with too much deference. Cousin Elizabeth, you
will have the honor of seeing Lady Catherine on Sunday at
church and I need not say that you will be delighted with her.
She is all affability and condescension. But now, Sir William,
Maria, allow me to show you my garden, of which, I must
admit, quite proud.

(SIR WILLIAM and **MARIA** exit with **MR.
COLLINS**.)

CHARLOTTE

It is good to see you Elizabeth. I am glad you came.

ELIZABETH

I thank you for the invitation, Charlotte. This is a lovely room.

CHARLOTTE

I am fond of it and spend much of my time here. Mr. Collins prefers to spend time in his study or in his garden.

ELIZABETH

Gardening is a healthful exercise.

CHARLOTTE

Yes, indeed, and I encourage him in it as much as possible. Between his study and his gardening I find it is possible to go much of the day without see him at all. Pray be seated. What do you hear from Jane in London?

ELIZABETH

It is much as I feared. She called upon Miss Bingley, but was received quite coolly. She has resolved to continue their acquaintance no longer.

CHARLOTTE

I am sorry to hear of it.

ELIZABETH

Yes, but perhaps it is just as well. Miss Bingley seems to admire where it is convenient.

CHARLOTTE

And what of you and Mr. Wickham? Shall there be an announcement soon?

ELIZABETH

I'm sure there shall be an announcement regarding Mr.
Wickham, but I shan't be a party to it. Before I left
Longbourn, the news came that Mr. Wickham is soon to be
engaged to a Miss King who, as Mrs. Philips told Mama, has
inherited ten thousand pounds. Please do not be sad for me,
for I am now convinced that I have never been much in love.
Kitty and Lydia took his defection much more to heart than I
do. They are young in the ways of the world, and do not
comprehend that handsome young men must have something
to live on, as well as the plain.

CHARLOTTE

Pray excuse me, I must ask Mr. Collins for some herbs for
supper.

(**CHARLOTTE** exits. A moment later
MARIA enters, running.)

MARIA

Oh, my dear Elizabeth! Pray, make haste and come to the
window, for there is such a sight to be seen!

(The two girls cross to the window, where
MARIA pulls back the curtain.)

ELIZABETH

Is this all, Maria? It's merely a phaeton with two ladies
talking to Mr. Collins and your father. I had expected at least
that the pigs were into the garden.

MARIA

It is not merely two ladies; that is Miss Anne DeBourgh and
Mrs. Jenkinson, who lives with Miss Anne and Lady
Catherine.

ELIZABETH

She is abominably rude to keep Charlotte out of doors. Why does she not come in?

MARIA

She hardly ever does. It is the greatest of favors when she does. They are coming back in; perhaps they will tell us what Miss DeBourgh said to them.

ELIZABETH

She looks sickly and cross. Yes, she will do for him very well.

(**MR. COLLINS** and **SIR WILLIAM** enter, excited.)

MR. COLLINS

I confess I should not have been at all surprised by Her Ladyship's asking us to Rosings for tea on Sunday, but who could have foreseen such an attention as this?

SIR WILLIAM

Who indeed?

MARIA

What is it?

MR. COLLINS

We've been invited to dine at Rosings tonight.

MARIA

Oh my! Whatever shall we wear, Miss Elizabeth?

(**ELIZABETH** starts to respond, but **MR. COLLINS** interrupts.)

MR. COLLINS

Do not make yourself uneasy, my dear cousin, about your apparel. Lady Catherine is far from requiring that elegance of dress in others which becomes herself and her daughter and will not think the worse of you for being simply dressed. She likes to have the distinction of rank preserved.

(BLACKOUT)

ACT I

Scene 10

SETTING: A parlor in Rosings.

AT RISE: **LADY CATHERINE** is seated in a
chair, with the party from the parsonage seated
opposite or standing.

MR. COLLINS
Lady Catherine, I have never had a better supper set before
me. The lamb was done to perfection!

SIR WILLIAM
I must agree with Mr. Collins, ma'am. The sauce that
accompanied it was quite delicious.

LADY CATHERINE
I shall have any of the food that is left from supper sent to
your home, Mrs. Collins. I refuse to eat old food, but there is
no reason it should go to waste.

MRS. COLLINS
You are most kind, Lady Catherine.

MR. COLLINS
Most kind indeed. As I was telling Sir William...

LADY CATHERINE
(Interrupts)
Mrs. Collins, your friend is a genteel, pretty kind of girl.

ELIZABETH
Thank you ma'am.

LADY CATHERINE
How many sisters have you?

ELIZABETH
I have an older sister and three younger sisters.

LADY CATHERINE
Do you or any of your sisters play and sing, Miss Bennet?

ELIZABETH
I have little ability, but I have a sister who loves to play and sing.

LADY CATHERINE
Why did you not all learn? Do any of you draw?

ELIZABETH
No, not at all.

LADY CATHERINE
What, none of you? That is very strange. Has your governess left you?

ELIZABETH
We never had any governess.

LADY CATHERINE
No governess! How was that possible with five daughters? Your education must have been neglected.

ELIZABETH
Compared with some families, I believe we were. But such of us as wished to learn never were encouraged to read and had all the masters as necessary. Those who chose to be idle certainly might.

LADY CATHERINE

Aye, no doubt; but that is what a governess will prevent. If I
had known your mother, I should have advised her most
strenuously to engage one. Mrs. Collins, did I tell you of Lady
Metcalf's calling to thank me for helping her find a governess?
"Lady Catherine," said she, "you have given me a treasure."
Are any of your sisters out, Miss Bennet?

ELIZABETH

Yes, ma'am, all.

LADY CATHERINE

What, all five out at once? The younger ones out before the
elder are married? Your younger sisters must be very young.

ELIZABETH

My youngest sister is not sixteen. Perhaps she is full young to
be much in company. But really, ma'am, I think it would be
very hard upon younger sisters that they should not have
their share of society because the elder may not have the
means nor the inclination to marry.

LADY CATHERINE

Upon my word, you give your opinion very decidedly for so
young a person. Pray, what is your age?

ELIZABETH

With three younger sisters grown up, Your Ladyship can
hardly expect me to own it.

LADY CATHERINE

You cannot be more than twenty, I am sure.

ELIZABETH

I am not twenty and one.

LADY CATHERINE
My niece, Miss Georgiana Darcy is but sixteen. Darcy will see
to her presentation next spring. I am sure we will discuss at
length, for he depends upon my advice.
(Looks at **ELIZABETH**.)
Hmmmm...

SERVANT
(Enters. Bows.)
Mr. Darcy and Colonel Fitzwilliam.

(The gentlemen enter as the Parsonage party
stands. **SERVANT** exits. Bows/curtsies.
LADY CATHERINE gestures all of them to
tables set for cards. They begin to play.)

COL. FITZWILLIAM
I am glad to finally have made your acquaintance, Miss
Bennet. I have heard so much about you.

MR. DARCY
Is your family well?

ELIZABETH
They are quite well, I thank you. My elder sister has been in
town these three months. Have you never happened to see
her?

MR. DARCY
(Uncomfortable.)
I was not so fortunate as to see Miss Bennet.

MR. COLLINS
We are most grieved to hear that Miss DeBourgh is feeling
unwell this evening.

LADY CATHERINE
We called the doctor and he said that several days of bed rest would do the trick.

CHARLOTTE
Please convey our best wishes for Miss DeBourgh's recovery.

MR. COLLINS AND SIR WILLIAM
(Ad lib.)
Indeed yes, a speedy recovery, our evening was bereft of true pleasure, etc.

LADY CATHERINE
(Looks at the other table.)
What is that you are saying Fitzwilliam? What are you telling Miss Bennet? Let me hear what it is.

COL. FITZWILLIAM
We are speaking of music, madam.

LADY CATHERINE
Ah, music. There are few people who have more true enjoyment of music than myself. If I had ever learnt, I should have been a great proficient. How does Georgiana get on with her music, Darcy?

MR. DARCY
Her ability grows and her music master is quite pleased with her progress.

LADY CATHERINE
I am very glad to hear; pray tell her from me, that she cannot expect to excel if she does not practice a great deal. I have told Miss Bennet that she will never play really well, unless she practices more. Though Mrs. Collins has no instrument, she is welcome to come to Rosings every day and play on the pianoforte in Mrs. Jenkinson's room. She would be in nobody's

way in that part of the house.

> (Both **MR. DARCY** and **COL.**
> **FITZWILLIAM** are embarrassed by **LADY**
> **CATHERINE'S** rude comments.)

COL. FITZWILLIAM
Miss Bennet, Darcy told me that you and he met at a dance in Hertfordshire.

ELIZABETH
Col. Fitzwilliam, I fear your cousin will give you a pretty notion of our life in Hertfordshire. Indeed, Mr. Darcy, it is very ungenerous of you and it is provoking me to retaliate with such things may come out as will shock your relations to hear.

MR. DARCY
I am not afraid of you.

COL. FITZWILLIAM
Pray let me hear what you have to accuse him of. I should like to know how he behaved among strangers.

ELIZABETH
You shall hear then. The first time of my ever seeing him in Hertfordshire was at a ball, where he danced only four dances, though gentlemen were scarce and more than one young lady was sitting down in want of a partner.

MR. DARCY
I had not the honor of knowing any lady beyond my own party and I am ill qualified to recommend myself to strangers.

ELIZABETH
Col. Fitzwilliam, shall we ask your cousin why a man of sense and education is ill qualified to recommend himself to

strangers?

COL. FITZWILLIAM
It is because he will not give himself the trouble.

MR. DARCY
I have not the talent which some people possess of conversing easily with those I have never seen before.

ELIZABETH
As Lady Catherine will tell you, my hands do not move over the pianoforte in a masterly manner; but then I have always supposed it to be my own fault because I would not take the trouble of practicing.

MR. DARCY
You have employed your time much better. No one admitted to the privilege of hearing you can think anything wanting.

> (They concentrate on their game for a moment. **MARIA** wins and crosses to the other table where she switches with her father and begins to play. **MR. DARCY** follows to watch. **ELIZABETH** gets up and crosses to the window and **COL. FITZWILLIAM** joins her.)

COL. FITZWILLIAM
Are you enjoying the scenery?

ELIZABETH
I am indeed. It's beautiful.

COL. FITZWILLIAM
Rosings is nothing if not beautiful.

ELIZABETH
Will you remain at Rosings long, Colonel Fitzwilliam?

COL. FITZWILLIAM
Yes, if Darcy does not decide otherwise. I am at his disposal.

ELIZABETH
I imagine your cousin brought you down with him chiefly for the sake of having somebody at his disposal. I wonder he does not marry to secure a lasting convenience of that kind; but perhaps his sister, being under his care, does as well for the present.

COL. FITZWILLIAM
No, that is an advantage which he must divide with me. I am joined in the guardianship of Miss Darcy. Are you acquainted with her?

ELIZABETH
I am not, although she is the favorite of some ladies of my acquaintance, Mrs. Hurst and Miss Bingley.

COL. FITZWILLIAM
I know them a little. Their brother is a pleasant gentleman and a great friend of Darcy.

ELIZABETH
Oh, yes, Mr. Darcy is uncommonly kind to Mr. Bingley and takes a prodigious deal of care of him.

COL. FITZWILLIAM
(Laughs.)
Yes, I do believe Darcy *does* take care of him. I gather that Bingley has reason to be very much indebted to him. Darcy congratulated himself on having lately saved him from a most imprudent marriage.

ELIZABETH

Indeed? And did Mr. Darcy give you his reasons for this
interference?

COL. FITZWILLIAM

I understood that there were some very strong objections
against the lady.

ELIZABETH

Why was Mr. Darcy to be the judge? What right had he to
direct in what manner his friend was to be happy? Perhaps
there was not much affection in the case.

COL. FITZWILLIAM

That is not an unnatural surmise, but it would lessen the
honor of my cousin's triumph very sadly.

(BLACKOUT)

ACT I

Scene 11

SETTING: The Collins' parlor.

AT RISE: **ELIZABETH** is reading letters, when
she hears the door bell. She stands and smoothes her
hair when the **MAID** enters.

MAID
(Curtsey.)
Mr. Darcy, mum.

(**MR. DARCY** enters. Bows/curtsies.)

MR. DARCY
I was sorry to learn that you were not coming to Rosings
today. I understand from Mrs. Collins that you were unwell?

ELIZABETH
Yes, I had a headache and felt that a quiet afternoon would
ease the pain.

(She gestures to a chair and they both sit.
After a moment, he gets up and walks about
the room. He turns to her.)

MR. DARCY
In vain have I struggled, but my feelings will not be
repressed. You must allow me to tell you how ardently I
admire and love you. I realize that there are some obstacles,
the sense of your inferiority, your family's status; it goes
against everything in my will, my reason, and even my
character. But I am determined to overlook them if you will
do me the honor of becoming my wife.

ELIZABETH
(Startled.)
In such cases as this, it is, I believe, the established mode to express a sense of obligation for the sentiments avowed. However, I cannot – I have never desired your good opinion, and you have certainly bestowed it most unwillingly. I am sorry to have occasioned pain to any one; it has been unconsciously done, however and I hope will be of short duration.

MR. DARCY
And this is all the reply which I am to expect? I might, perhaps, wish to be informed why, with so little endeavor at civility, I am rejected.

ELIZABETH
I might as well enquire why, with so evident a design of offending and insulting me, you chose to tell me that you liked me against your will, against your reason, and even against your character? Was not this some excuse for incivility? Had not my own feelings been decided against you, do you think that any consideration would tempt me to accept the man who has been the means of ruining the happiness of a most beloved sister?... Can you deny that you have done it?

MR. DARCY
I have no wish to deny that I did everything in my power to separate my friend from your sister.

ELIZABETH
But it is not merely that affair. Long before it had taken place, my opinion of you was decided. Your character was unfolded in the recital from Mr. Wickham. On this subject what can you say?

MR. DARCY
You take an eager interest in that gentlemen's concerns.

ELIZABETH

Who, knowing his misfortunes, can help but have an interest
in him?

MR. DARCY

His misfortunes! Yes, they have been great indeed.

ELIZABETH

And of your infliction. You have withheld the advantages
which you must know to have been designed for him. And yet
you treat his misfortunes with contempt and ridicule.

MR. DARCY

And this is your opinion of me? My faults, according to this
calculation, are heavy indeed. Perhaps these offenses might
have been overlooked had not your pride been hurt by my
honest confession of the scruples that had prevented my
forming any serious design. But disguise of every sort is my
abhorrence. Nor am I ashamed of the feeling I related. They
are natural and just. Could you expect me to rejoice in the
inferiority of your connections?

ELIZABETH

You are mistaken, Mr. Darcy, if you suppose that the mode of
your declaration affected me in any other way than as it
spared me the concern which I might have felt in refusing
you, had you behaved in a more gentleman-like manner. You
could not have made me the offer of your hand in any possible
way that would have tempted me to accept it. I had not
known you a month before I felt that you were the last man in
the world whom I could ever be prevailed on to marry.

MR. DARCY

You have said quite enough, madam. I perfectly comprehend
your feelings and have now only to be ashamed of what my
own have been. Forgive me for having taken up so much of
your time and accept my best wishes for your health and

happiness.

(Bows and exits.)

(BLACKOUT)

ACT I

Scene 12

SETTING: On one side of the stage is a desk and
chair at the parsonage. On the other side is a desk
and chair at Rosings.

AT RISE: **ELIZABETH** enters on the parsonage
side, carrying a folded letter. **MR. DARCY** enters on
the Rosings side, clearly upset. He ponders for a
moment.

MR. DARCY
I will be justified!

> (**MR. DARCY** sits at the desk and begins
> writing. He either reads aloud while he writes
> or reads through a pre-recorded voiceover.
> **ELIZABETH** opens the letter and reads.)

MR. DARCY/VOICEOVER
Be not alarmed, madam, on receiving this letter, by the
apprehension of its containing any repetition of those
sentiments, or the renewal of those offers, which were last
night so disgusting to you.

There were two offenses you laid to my charge. The first was
that – regardless of the feelings of either – I had detached Mr.
Bingley from your sister. The other, that I had, in defiance to
honor, ruined the prosperity and prospects of Mr. Wickham.
From the severity of that blame I shall hope to be secured
when the following account of my actions and motives are
revealed.

ELIZABETH
(Reading aloud.)

At the dance at Netherfield I first became acquainted that Bingley's attention to your sister had given rise to a general expectation of their marriage. From that moment, I observed my friend's behavior and could see that his partiality for her was evident. I also observed your sister and noted from her countenance that, though she received his attentions with pleasure, her heart was not touched. If I have wounded your sister's feelings, it was unknowingly done.

MR. DARCY/VOICEOVER
With respect to Mr. Wickham, I can only lay before you the whole of his connection with my family.

Mr. Wickham is the son of a very respectable man, who had the management of all the Pemberley estates. My father was godfather to George Wickham and had the highest opinion of the young man; hoping the church would be his profession, my father intended to provide for it. But his vicious propensities and want of principle, which he carefully guarded from our fathers, could not escape my observation.

My excellent father died about five years ago as did the elder Mr. Wickham. Within half a year, Mr. Wickham wrote to inform me that he resolved against taking orders and did not think it unreasonable for him to expect a monetary settlement, with the intention, he said, of studying the law. I wished – rather than believed him – to be sincere and sent him funds in the amount of three thousand pounds.

His study of the law was a mere pretense and now being free from all restraint, his life was idleness and dissipation.

ELIZABETH
(Reading aloud.)
Last summer my sister went with her companion, Mrs. Young, to Ramsgate; there also, went Mr. Wickham, undoubtedly by design. Georgiana, whose impression of Mr.

Wickham's kindness to her as a child, was soon persuaded to believe herself in love and to consent to an elopement. She was then but fifteen.

I joined them unexpectedly a day before the intended elopement and Georgiana, acknowledged the whole to me. You may imagine what I felt. Mr. Wickham's chief object was unquestionably my sister's fortune, which is thirty thousand pounds.

This, madam, is a faithful narrative and you will. For the truth of everything related here, I can appeal to the testimony of Colonel Fitzwilliam, who has been acquainted with the particulars of these transactions. I will only add, God bless you.

(BLACKOUT)

INTERMISSION

ACT II

Scene 1

SETTING: The Bennet Parlor.

AT RISE: The Bennet family is present.

MR. BENNET
I am glad you are come back, Jane. Lizzy. You were missed.

KITTY
You should have seen them when they found that we were meeting them. Oh Mary, you should have come with us.

MARY
Far be it from me to depreciate such pleasures. They would doubtless be congenial with the generality of female minds, but I confess I should infinitely prefer a book.

KITTY
We had ordered a cold luncheon; but Jane and Lizzy had to lend us money, for we had spent all ours at the shop.

LYDIA
I bought this bonnet. I did not think it pretty, but I thought I might as well buy it as not.
                    (Sudden pout.)
Besides, it will not signify what one wears this summer. What do you think, Lizzy, Jane, the militia is to leave Meryton.

KITTY
They are going to be encamped near Brighton.

LYDIA
I should love Brighton, but Papa will not take us.

MRS. BENNET
A little sea-bathing would set me up forever.

MR. BENNET
I refuse to be convinced.

LYDIA
Lizzy, Wickham is safe. There's no danger of his marrying Mary King. She is gone to her uncle at Liverpool.

JANE
I hope there is no strong attachment on either side.

LYDIA
I am sure there is not on his side. Who could care about such a little freckled thing?

MR. BENNET
I will leave you now; I have a new book awaiting me in my study.
(He exits.)

MRS. BENNET
I am going to lie down before supper. I must say I enjoy a quiet evening at home now and then.
(She exits.)

LYDIA
Come Kitty, let us change and walk to Meryton. Perhaps there is news of the militia.

MARY
I am going to my room and continue my study of Fordyce's.

(**MARY**, **LYDIA** and **KITTY** exit.)

JANE
(Waits for them to be alone.)
I cannot believe Mr. Darcy proposed to you. His manner of delivering his sentiments was wrong, but only consider how much it must increase his disappointment.

ELIZABETH
You do not blame me for refusing him?

JANE
Blame you? Oh no! But his tale of Mr. Wickham. How could that much wickedness exist in one individual? Perhaps there was an error of understanding on both sides.

ELIZABETH
This will not do, Jane, you will never be able to make both of them good. For my part, I am inclined to believe Mr. Darcy.

JANE
Lizzy, only consider what Mr. Darcy must have suffered having to relate such a thing of his sister.

ELIZABETH
I confess I was very uncomfortable and with no Jane to comfort me... There is one point on which I want your advice. Whether or not to make our acquaintance understand Wickham's character.

JANE
Surely there can be occasion for exposing him so dreadfully. What is your opinion?

ELIZABETH
That it ought not to be attempted. Mr. Darcy has not authorized me to make his communication public. With the regiment leaving, Mr. Wickham will soon be gone. Therefore, it will not signify to anybody here what he really is.

JANE
You are quite right. To have his errors made public might
ruin him forever. Perhaps he is now sorry for what he has
done and anxious to re-established his character.

> (**LYDIA** and **KITTY** enter. **LYDIA** is calling
> for their parents. **MR.** and **MRS. BENNET**
> enter a moment later.)

LYDIA
You will never guess! Mrs. Forester has invited me to
accompany her to Brighton. Colonel Forester said that I
would keep his wife company.

KITTY
I cannot see why Mrs. Forester should not ask me as well as
Lydia, I have just as much right as she has – and more too –
for I am two years older.

MRS. BENNET
Oh Lydia! What good fortune for you! And such
condescension. You must not neglect any opportunity of
enjoying yourself.

LYDIA
I certainly shall enjoy myself. Mama I shall need all new
clothes.

MRS. BENNET
Of course, you shall, my dear. Come, let's go to your room and
see what you need. Jane, go and ask Hill to prepare Lydia's
favorite dishes for supper, to celebrate.

> (**JANE**, **KITTY**, **MRS. BENNET**, and
> **LYDIA** exit.)

ELIZABETH

Father, are you going to allow this?

MR. BENNET

I see no reason not to. Lydia has been making the household miserable with her repining over Brighton. Now she is going and Colonel Forester will have to put up with her silliness.

ELIZABETH

Father, away from home, Lydia will be yet more imprudent.

MR. BENNET

Lydia will never be easy 'til she has exposed herself in some public place.

ELIZABETH

If you were aware of the great disadvantage to us all, which has already arisen from Lydia's unguarded and imprudent manner...

MR. BENNET

Already arisen? What? Has she frightened away some of your lovers, Lizzy?

ELIZABETH

Indeed you are mistaken. I have no such injuries. Excuse me for speaking plainly, but if you will not check her exuberant spirits, her character will be fixed as the most determined flirt that has ever made herself and her family ridiculous.

MR. BENNET

Do not make yourself uneasy, my love. Wherever you and Jane are known, you must be respected and valued. No, we shall have no peace at Longbourn if Lydia does not go to Brighton. You are to go with your Aunt and Uncle Gardiner to the lake country; let Lydia go with the Foresters. Colonel Forester is a sensible man and will keep her out of any real mischief.

(BLACKOUT)

ACT II

Scene 2

SETTING: A parlor at Pemberley.

AT RISE: **MR.** and **MRS. GARDINER** and
ELIZABETH are standing near the door.

MR. GARDINER
Your Aunt Gardiner and I are pleased that you were able to
come with us on our tour of Derbyshire.

ELIZABETH
I thank you for your invitation, Uncle Gardiner. I understand,
Aunt, that you spent time here as a young girl?

MRS. GARDINER
Yes, some of the happiest days of my childhood were spent in
Lambton. And in all that time, I never had the privilege of
seeing Pemberley, although I heard much of its beauty. I look
forward to seeing it.

ELIZABETH
Are we certain that the family is away? I would never wish to
impose on their privacy.

MR. GARDINER
The housekeeper, Mrs. Reynolds assured me that the family
is indeed away and that she would be most pleased to show us
the house.

(**MRS. REYNOLDS** enters.)

MRS. REYNOLDS
Welcome to Pemberley, sir, ma'am.

MR. GARDINER

Thank you, Mrs. Reynolds. This is my wife, Mrs. Gardiner and our niece, Elizabeth Bennet.
>   (Curtsies.)

MRS. REYNOLDS

I understand you wish to see Pemberley? Please come this way.

MR. GARDINER

Yes, indeed. What a handsome room.

MRS. REYNOLDS

This is the blue parlor; the family prefers this room during the summer.

ELIZABETH

And the family; we understood they are away at present.

MRS. REYNOLDS

Yes, they are, although we expect the master tomorrow with a large party.

MRS. GARDINER
>   (Looking at several miniature pictures above
>   the mantel.)

Lizzy, do come and look. Is this not Mr. Wickham?

>   (They cross to her.)

MRS. REYNOLDS

Aye, that is indeed Mr. Wickham, the son of my late master's steward. He's now gone into the army, but I am afraid he has turned out very wild.
>   (Points to a picture of **MR. DARCY**.)

And that is my master and very like him.

MRS. GARDINER
It is a handsome face. But Lizzy, you can tell us whether it is like him or not.

MRS. REYNOLDS
Does this young lady know Mr. Darcy?

ELIZABETH
A little.

MRS. REYNOLDS
Do not you think him a very handsome gentleman?

ELIZABETH
Yes, very handsome.

MRS. GARDINER
Is Miss Darcy as handsome as her brother?

MRS. REYNOLDS
Oh yes, the handsomest young lady as ever was seen. And so accomplished; she plays and sings all day long. In the next room is a new instrument just come down – a present to her from my master.

MR. GARDNER
What a generous and kind thing to do.

MRS. REYNOLDS
I have never had a cross word from him in my life and I have known him since he was four years old. But I have always observed that, they who are good-natured when children, are good-natured when they grow up. He is the best landlord and the best master. Some people call him proud, but I am sure I never saw anything of it. If you will excuse me a moment, I must speak with the cook.
                    (MRS. REYNOLDS exits.)

MR. GARDINER
Yes, of course.

MRS. GARDINER
That was a fine account of Mr. Darcy; not what we had supposed.

ELIZABETH
Perhaps we might have been deceived.

>   (**MR.** and **MRS. GARDINER** cross to the
>   other side of the room when **MR. DARCY**
>   enters. He and **ELIZABETH** are both
>   shocked to see each other.)

MR. DARCY
Miss Bennet.
>   (Bows/curtsies.)

ELIZABETH
Mr. Darcy. We had no idea you were expected today. We inquired of the housekeeper and were informed that the family was not expected before tomorrow. We would never have presumed upon your privacy.

MR. DARCY
Yes. Well. I have business with my steward and thought to come before the rest of my party... How long have you been in Derbyshire?

ELIZABETH
Only a few days.

MR. DARCY
And where are you staying?

ELIZABETH

The inn at Lambton.

MR. DARCY

Yes, of course... Well, if you will excuse me.
(Bows and exits.)

(**MR.** and **MRS. GARDINER** cross to
ELIZABETH.)

MR. GARDINER

The gentleman himself, I presume?

MRS. GARDINER

He is certainly as handsome as his portrait.

ELIZABETH
(Upset; pacing.)
Oh, I wish we'd never come here!

(**ELIZABETH** paces towards the far side of
the Stage; **MR.** and **MRS. GARDINER**
follow.)

MR. GARDINER

What?

ELIZABETH

What he must think of me!

MRS. GARDINER

I thought you cared not for his opinion.

ELIZABETH

I don't! I mean, I do. I mean...oh, I don't know what I mean.

MRS. GARDINER
I can see that.

ELIZABETH
We must leave at once!

MR. GARDINER
Leave? Do you mean leave Lambton?

ELIZABETH
Yes, and as soon as may be possible.

MRS. GARDINER
My dear, you must calm yourself and explain your reasonings.

ELIZABETH
I can't. I mean...

(**MR. DARCY** enters.)

MR. DARCY
Miss Bennet.
(He crosses to **ELIZABETH**.)
You're not leaving are you?

ELIZABETH
I think we must.

MR. DARCY
It's not because of Pemberley, is it?

ELIZABETH
No, indeed.

MR. DARCY
Then you do like it?

ELIZABETH

Yes, I do. Pemberley is the most beautiful of estates.

MR. DARCY

I'm glad to hear it; for your good opinion is most desirable...
Would you please do me the honor of introducing your
friends?

ELIZABETH

Oh yes, of course. Mr. Darcy, this is my aunt and uncle, Mr.
and Mrs. Gardiner.

(They bow/curtsey.)

MR. GARDINER

Sir, you have a handsome estate.

MRS. GARDINER

Yes, indeed. I heard that Pemberley was the one of the most
beautiful estates in of Derbyshire, but that praise did not do it
justice.

MR. DARCY

I thank you. Are you familiar with Derbyshire?

MRS. GARDINER

I grew up in Lambton.

MR. DARCY

I spent many a day as a young boy running to Lambton. A
delightful village. Mr. Gardiner, do you fish?

MR. GARDINER

I do indeed, sir.

MR. DARCY

Then you must come and fish in my stream. My man will
supply you with fishing tackle. Miss Bennet; among those

who are coming are some who will claim an acquaintance
with you – Mr. Bingley and his sisters.

ELIZABETH
Indeed?

MR. DARCY
There is also one other person who more particularly wishes
to be known to you; my sister, Georgiana. Would you allow me
the honor of introducing her to you?

ELIZABETH
I would be most honored to meet Miss Darcy.

MR. DARCY
Thank you.
> (Turning to **MR. GARDINER**.)

Come sir, let me point out some of the best fishing spots.
> (The men exit.)

MRS. GARDINER
Well, Mr. Darcy is not at all the way he was described.

ELIZABETH
> (Looking after **MR. DARCY**.)

No indeed. I wonder what could have caused the change?

MRS. GARDINER
Do you indeed?

(BLACKOUT)

ACT II

Scene 3

SETTING: A parlor at Pemberley.

AT RISE: **MR. DARCY, MR. BINGLEY, MRS. HURST, MISS BINGLEY, MRS. GARDINER, GEORGIANA** and **ELIZABETH** are present.

GEORGIANA
It's a pleasure to meet you, Miss Bennet. I have heard much about you.

ELIZABETH
I do hope that what you have heard was kind.

GEORGIANA
Indeed it was most kind, Miss Bennet, for I heard it from my brother. Mrs. Gardiner, I am so glad you could come as well. May I present Mrs. Hurst and Miss Bingley and their brother, Mr. Bingley?

(Curtsies and bows.)

MRS. GARDINER
Mr. Darcy, it was kind of you to invite my husband to come and fish in your stream this morning. He could talk of nothing else over breakfast.

MR. DARCY
I was most happy to oblige him.

ELIZABETH
Mr. Bingley, it's a pleasure to see you again.

MR. BINGLEY
Miss Bennet. What a pleasure to see you... How is your

family?

ELIZABETH
They are well, I thank you.

MR. BINGLEY
And are *all* your sisters at home?

ELIZABETH
Yes, Mr. Bingley, they are.

MR. BINGLEY
I can't believe how long it has been since last we saw each other. It is above eight months, when we were all dancing together at Netherfield.

MISS BINGLEY
(Cold.)
And how is your family, Miss Elizabeth Bennet?

ELIZABETH
(Equally as cold.)
They are all well, I thank you.

GEORGIANA
Would you please be seated? May I offer you some tea?

MRS. GARDINER
Thank you, that would be most pleasant.

(**GEORGIANA** crosses to sit behind the tea table. She pours tea for **MRS. GARDINER** who takes the cup and sits down.)

MR. DARCY
I understand from Mrs. Reynolds that you were not able to

see all of Pemberley. Georgiana or I would be most happy to
show you the rest.

GEORGIANA
Yes, indeed I would. Tea, Miss Bennet?
>   (Holds cup out to **ELIZABETH**.)

MISS BINGLEY
Pray, Miss Bennet, are not the militia removed from
Meryton? That must be a great loss to *your* family. I know
that one officer was an especial friend of yours; Mr. Wickham.

GEORGIANA
>   (**GEORGIANA'S** hand shakes; she spills tea
>   on **ELIZABETH'S** dress.)
Oh, Miss Bennet, I am so sorry. Pray forgive me.

ELIZABETH
No, Miss Darcy, it is you who must forgive me. I must have
been in your way.

GEORGIANA
But your dress.

ELIZABETH
It is nothing.

GEORGIANA
Pray let me take you to Mrs. Reynolds. I am certain she has
something that will prevent a stain.

MRS. GARDINER
I will come with you, Lizzy, for I know several recipes to
prevent stains.

>   (**ELIZABETH, GEORGIANA**, and **MRS.
>   GARDINER** exit.)

MISS BINGLEY

How very ill Eliza Bennet looks this morning. She is grown so
brown and coarse. I was just saying to Louisa that I would not
have recognized her.

MRS. HURST

Nor I.

MR. DARCY

I have perceived no other alteration than her being tanned –
the consequence of traveling in the summer.

MISS BINGLEY
(To **MRS. HURST**.)

For my own part, I must confess that I never could see any
beauty in her. Her face is too thin. Her complexion has no
brilliancy. Her features are not at all handsome. Her teeth
are tolerable, I suppose, but not out of the common. And as for
her eyes, which have sometimes been called fine, I never
could perceive anything extraordinary in them. And in her
air, there is a self-sufficiency without fashion, which is
intolerable.

I remember when we first knew her in Hertfordshire, how
amazed we were to find that she was a reputed beauty.
(To **MR. DARCY**.)

I particularly recall your saying one night, "*She* a beauty! I
should as soon call her mother a wit!"
(She and **MRS. HURST** laugh.)

But afterwards she seemed to improve on you and I believe
you thought her rather pretty.

MR. DARCY

Yes, but *that* was only when I first knew her. For it is many
months since I have considered her as one of the handsomest
women of my acquaintance.

(He bows and exits as **lights fade to black)**

ACT II

Scene 4

SETTING: The parlor at the inn.

AT RISE: **MR.** and **MRS. GARDINER** and
ELIZABETH are preparing to go out when the **MAID**
enters.

MAID
(Curtsies.)
Letters have arrived for you.
(Hands the letters to **ELIZABETH** and exits)

ELIZABETH
At last; a letter from Jane. No wonder it was delayed in
coming; the direction was written remarkable ill indeed.

MRS. GARDINER
I know you have longed for news from home. Why don't you
sit here and enjoy your letter? Your uncle and I will walk to
the church alone and call for you in an hour's time.

ELIZABETH
Thank you very much. You are too good.

(**MR.** and **MRS. GARDINER** exit.
ELIZABETH sits and begins to read. As she
reads, she gets more upset. She stands up,
obviously upset.)

ELIZABETH
Oh, where is my uncle?

(The **MAID** enters, followed by **MR. DARCY**.)

MAID
(Curtsies.)
Mr. Darcy, ma'am.
(Exits. **MR. DARCY, ELIZABETH**
bows/curtsies.)

ELIZABETH
(Clearly distraught.)
I beg your pardon, but I must find my uncle this moment. I
have not an instant to lose.

MR. DARCY
What ever is the matter? I will not detain you, but let me – or
the servant – go after Mr. and Mrs. Gardiner.
(Crosses to the edge of the stage and calls
offstage.)
You, girl!
(The **MAID** enters.)
Send at once for Mr. and Mrs. Gardiner. They walked in the
direction of...
(Looks at **ELIZABETH**.)

ELIZABETH
The church.

MAID
(Curtsies.)
Right away, sir; ma'am.
(Exits.)

MR. DARCY
Is there nothing more I can do? Shall I get you a glass of
wine?

ELIZABETH
No, I thank you. I am only distressed by some dreadful news

which I have just received from Longbourn.

(She cries, then pauses and continues.)

My youngest sister has left all her friends and has...eloped. She has thrown herself into the power of-of Mr. Wickham. *You* know him too well to doubt the rest. She is lost forever. When I consider that *I* might have prevented it. Had his character been known, this could not have happened. But it is too late.

MR. DARCY

Is it certain?

(ELIZABETH nods.)

And what has been attempted to recover her?

ELIZABETH

My father is gone to London and Jane has written to beg my uncle's immediate assistance. But nothing can be done. How is such a man to be worked on? I have not the smallest hope.

MR. DARCY

(Uncomfortable pause.)

I am afraid you have been long desiring my absence. This unfortunate affair will, I fear, prevent my sister from having the pleasure of seeing you at Pemberley today.

ELIZABETH

(Stands.)

Oh, yes. Be so kind as to apologize for us to Miss Darcy. Conceal the unhappy truth as long as possible, although I know it can't be long.

(Bows and curtsies.)

I will never see him again.

(BLACKOUT)

ACT II

Scene 5

SETTING: The Bennet parlor.

AT RISE: **JANE** is present. **ELIZABETH** and
MR. and **MRS. GARDINER**.

ELIZABETH
Oh Jane. What news? Has anything been heard of Lydia?

JANE
Father wrote to say that he arrived safely and that he would
not write again 'til he had something of importance to
mention. But now that my uncle is come, I hope everything
will be well.

ELIZABETH
And Mother? How much you must have gone through.

JANE
But I know your presence will be of great comfort to her.

> (They cross to **MRS. BENNET**, who is on the
> far side of the stage, sitting in a chair with her
> feet propped up. She begins to cry.)

MRS. BENNET
Oh Lizzy. Oh Brother. Oh Sister. You have heard what that
villain Wickham has done? My poor Lydia. I am sure there
was some great neglect on the Forresters' part, for this would
not have happened if she had been well looked after. Now
here's Mr. Bennet gone away and I know he will fight
Wickham and will be killed and then what will become of us?
For I know the Collinses will turn us out and, if you are not
kind to us, Brother, I do know what we shall do.

MR. GARDINER

Now, sister, calm yourself. I mean to leave for London this very day to assist in the search.

MRS. BENNET

Oh, dear Brother, that is exactly what I wished for. When you do find them, if they are not married already, *make* them marry. And, above all, keep Mr. Bennet from fighting. Tell him what a dreadful state I am in – that I have such tremblings, such flutterings, such spasms in my side, and pains in my heart.

(Stops weeping.)

And tell Lydia not to give any directions about the wedding clothes till she has seen me, for she does not know which are the best warehouses.

MR. GARDINER

I will see about a fresh horse immediately.

(He exits.)

ELIZABETH

Mother, we will leave you to talk to our aunt. Jane and I will see to your tea.

(**MARY** and **KITTY** enter. **JANE** and **ELIZABETH** cross to the parlor as they enter.)

ELIZABETH

Mary; Kitty. It is good to see you.

KITTY

It is good to see you too, Lizzy. And it is good to have someone not speak to me as if this whole thing were my fault.

MARY

This is a most unfortunate affair, and will probably be much talked of. But we must stem the tide of malice and pour into the wounded bosoms of each other the balm of sisterly consolation. Unhappy as the event must be for Lydia, we may draw from it this useful lesson – that loss of virtue in a female is irretrievable, that her reputation is no less brittle than it is beautiful, and that she cannot be too much guarded towards the undeserving of the other sex.

JANE
Thank you, Mary.

ELIZABETH
Now Jane, tell me all that I have not already heard. Did anyone have an apprehension of anything concerning Lydia and Wickham?

JANE
Colonel Forester brought a letter that Lydia had written to his wife.
(She hands the note to **ELIZABETH**.)

ELIZABETH
(Reads.)
"My dear Harriet. You will laugh when you know where I am gone and I cannot help laughing myself at your surprise tomorrow morning when it is discovered that I am missed. I am gone to Gretna Green and, if you cannot guess with who, then I shall think you a simpleton. For there is but one man in the world I love. You need not send word to Longbourn, for it will make the surprise all the greater when I write to them and sign my name Lydia Wickham. What a good joke it will be."
(Looks up.)
Oh, thoughtless, thoughtless Lydia. What a letter to be written at such a moment.

JANE

But at least it shows that she was serious in the object of her journey.

(**HILL** enters.)

HILL

Mr. Collins, ma'am.

(The girls stand as **MR. COLLINS** enters. Bows/curtsies.)

MR. COLLINS

My dear cousins. I have come to condole with your parents.

JANE

Our father is in town and our mother is unwell.

MR. COLLINS

Ah. Well then...

(The girls sit. He remains standing, striking a sermonizing pose.)

I had come to condole on the grievous affliction you are all now suffering under.

JANE

Thank you, sir.

MR. COLLINS

Be assured, ladies, that Mrs. Collins and myself sincerely sympathize with you. The death of your sister would have been a blessing in comparison. It is more to be lamented, as my dear Charlotte informs me, that this licentiousness of behavior in your sister has proceeded from a faulty degree of indulgence. However that may be, you are grievously to be pitied.

MARY
We are very grateful, sir, for...

(**MR. COLLINS** interrupts.)

MR. COLLINS
...in which opinion I am joined by Lady Catherine DeBourgh,
to whom I related the whole affair. She agrees with me in
apprehending that this false step in one sister will be
injurious to the fortunes of all the others. For who, as Lady
Catherine condescendingly says, will connect themselves with
such a family?
(He starts to sit but, when **ELIZABETH**
stands, he straightens again.)

ELIZABETH
Who indeed, sir? We would understand if you were to feel it
unwise to stay any longer now. A clergyman can never be too
careful – especially one who enjoys the patronage of Lady
Catherine DeBourgh.

MR. COLLINS
Your thoughtfulness does you credit, Cousin Elizabeth.
(He crosses to the door.)
I am very, very sorry for you all.
(**MR. COLLINS** bows and exits.)

(BLACKOUT)

ACT II

Scene 6

SETTING: The Bennet parlor.

AT RISE: **JANE, KITTY, ELIZABETH** and **MARY** are present. **MR. BENNET** enters from the direction of **MRS. BENNET'S** room.

MR. BENNET
Jane, Lizzy, Kitty, Mary.

ELIZABETH
Father, what you must have endured...

MR. BENNET
Say nothing of that. Who should suffer but myself? It has been my own doing and I ought to feel it.

ELIZABETH
You must not be too severe upon yourself.

MR. BENNET
No, Lizzy, let me once in my life feel how much I have been to blame. Do not worry, I am not afraid of being overpowered; it will pass away soon enough.

JANE
Do you suppose Lydia and Mr. Wickham to be in London?

MR. BENNET
Where else can they be so well concealed?

KITTY
Lydia always wanted to go to London.

MR. BENNET
She is happy then and her residence there will probably be of some duration.

MARY
(Crosses to the tea tray.)
I must take tea up to Mother.

MR. BENNET
Still keeping to her room, eh? It gives such an elegance to our misfortune. Another day I will do the same, I will sit in my library, in my nightcap and powdering gown and give as much trouble as I can – or perhaps I may defer it 'til Kitty runs away.

KITTY
If I should ever go to Brighton, Papa, I would behave better than Lydia.

MR. BENNET
(Explodes.)
Go to Brighton?! I would not trust you so near it as East Bourne, for fifty pounds. No, Kitty. I have at last learnt to be cautious, and you will feel the effects of it. No officer is ever to enter my house again. Balls will be absolutely prohibited, unless you stand up with one of your sisters. And you are never to stir out of doors, 'til you can prove that you have spent ten minutes of every day in a rational manner.
(**KITTY** begins to tear up. Seeing her weep,
MR. BENNET appears to soften and pats her shoulder.)
Well, well, do not make yourself unhappy. If you are a good girl for the next ten years, I will take you to a review at the end of them.

(**KITTY** cries and runs from the room.)

ELIZABETH

Father, have you had any news from my uncle?

MR. BENNET

Yes, a letter arrived from him this morning.

JANE

What news? Good or bad?

MR. BENNET

What is there of good to expect.

(Hands her the letter.)

Here, perhaps you would like to read it. Read it aloud, for I hardly know myself what it is about.

ELIZABETH

"My dear brother, At last I am able to send you tidings of my niece, and such as I hope will give you satisfaction. I have seen them..."

JANE

They are married!

ELIZABETH

"They are not married, but if you are willing to perform the engagements which I ventured to make on your behalf, I hope it will not be long before they are." What engagements, Father?

MR. BENNET

Read on.

ELIZABETH

"To allow your daughter one hundred pounds per annum, of which I am happy to say, there will be some money to settle on my niece, even when Wickham's debts are discharged. We have judged it best that my niece be married from our home.

Send back your answer as soon as you can."
(Looks up from the letter.)
Can it possible that he will marry her?

JANE
Wickham is not so undeserving then, as we have thought.

ELIZABETH
Does our mother know?

MR. BENNET
I informed her before I came to you.

ELIZABETH
Have you answered the letter?

MR. BENNET
No, but it must be done soon.

ELIZABETH
But the terms, I suppose, must be complied with?

MR. BENNET
Complied with? Wickham's a fool if he takes her with a
farthing less than ten thousand pounds.

ELIZABETH
Ten thousand pounds? Heavens forbid. And yet they must
marry.

MR. BENNET
Yes, yes, they must marry. But there are two things that I
want very much to know – how much money your uncle has
laid down to bring it about and how am I ever to repay him?

(**MRS. BENNET, MARY** and **KITTY** enter.

KITTY is wiping her eyes. **MRS. BENNET** is quite excited.)

MRS. BENNET

Jane, Lizzy, you have heard the news? My dear, dear Lydia will be married! This is delightful indeed. My good, kind brother; I knew he would manage everything. How I long to see her – and dear Wickham too. But the clothes! I must write my sister Gardiner about them directly.

JANE

Mother, we have presumed upon our uncle as is. We are persuaded that he has pledged himself to assist Mr. Wickham with money.

MRS. BENNET

Presumed! What nonsense! Who else should do it but her uncle? Well! I am so happy. Mrs. Wickham! How well that sounds.

KITTY

Do you think they will come to live in the neighborhood?

MARY

Where would they live?

MRS. BENNET

Hay Park might do, if the Gouldings would quit it. Or the great house at Stoke, if the drawing rooms were larger.

KITTY

What about Purvis Lodge?

MRS. BENNET

Not Purvis Lodge. The attics are dreadful.

MR. BENNET
Mrs. Bennet, before you take any, or all of these houses, let us
come to a right understanding. Into *one* house in this
neighborhood they shall never have admittance. Neither Mr.
nor Mrs. Wickham will ever step foot into Longbourn.

(BLACKOUT)

ACT II

Scene 7

SETTING: The Bennet's parlor.

AT RISE: The family, with the exception of
LYDIA, is there. **MRS. BENNET** and **KITTY** are
looking out the front window.

KITTY
Look, Mama! There's a carriage come to the house.

MRS. BENNET
Oh, it is them. They are come.
          (**LYDIA** and **MR. WICKHAM** enter. General
          ad lib greetings.)
Oh, my dear Lydia. How well you look. And you too,
Wickham. Oh, let me kiss your cheek, for now you are family.

MR. WICKHAM
You are all kindness, ma'am, sir, to welcome my wife and me
to your home. It does not seem so long ago that we were here.

LYDIA
It's been three months since I went to Brighton and so much
has happened. Good gracious! When I went away, I had no
idea of being married.

MRS. BENNET
Now, if you will excuse me, I must talk to Hill about supper.
We want it to be very special indeed, to celebrate your
marriage.
          (**MRS. BENNET** exits)

MR. WICKHAM
Sir, if you would be so good as to step outside, I would like to

show you my new curricle.

(**MR. WICKHAM** and **MR. BENNET** exit.)

LYDIA
Well, here I am at Longbourn again. And what do you think of my husband? Is not he a charming man? You must go to Brighton; I dare say I shall get husbands for you all.

ELIZABETH
I thank you for my share of the favor, but I do not particularly like your way of getting husbands.

KITTY
What was your wedding like?

LYDIA
I had hoped that all of Wickham's friends would come, and hold their swords for us to walk under. But they couldn't be spared from their duties. In the end, only my aunt and uncle were there. And Mr. Darcy.

ELIZABETH
Mr. Darcy?

LYDIA
Oh, yes. Someone had to stand up with Wickham.
(Covers her mouth.)
Gracious me! I quite forgot. It was supposed to be a secret and I promised them so faithfully.
(Shrugs and changes tone.)
Come with me to my room, Kitty, Mary, for I have gifts for all of you.

(**KITTY, LYDIA** and **MARY** exit.)

JANE
Why would Mr. Darcy be at Lydia's wedding?

ELIZABETH

I do not know.

(**HILL** enters and hands her a letter.)

It's a letter from our Aunt Gardiner.

JANE

What does she write?

ELIZABETH

Here...

(**ELIZABETH** hands the letter to **JANE**.)

JANE

"My dear niece; after my return from Longbourn, your uncle and I had an unexpected visitor; Mr. Darcy. He came to tell us that he had discovered Lydia and Mr. Wickham. Mr. Darcy imputed that it was due to his pride that Wickham's character was not known and felt it his duty to remedy the evil that had resulted. He refused to be persuaded by your uncle's arguments. Nothing was to be done that he did not do and your uncle – instead of helping his niece - was forced to take the credit of it."

Elizabeth, Mr. Darcy paid Mr. Wickham's debts and arranged for him to go into the northern regiment.

ELIZABETH

So it would seem.

(The Bennet family enters. **KITTY** is carrying a tea tray.)

MRS. BENNET

Hill has supper well in hand and has made Lydia's favorite cake for tea.

(She serves tea. **ELIZABETH** moves to the window. **MR. WICKHAM** follows.)

MR. WICKHAM
My dear sister, I learned from the Gardiners that you have
actually seen Pemberley?

ELIZABETH
Yes, I saw it when my aunt and uncle and I were at Lambton.

MR. WICKHAM
I almost envy you the pleasure... I was surprised to see Darcy
in town last month. I wonder what he can be doing there.

ELIZABETH
Perhaps preparing for his marriage to Miss DeBourgh.

MR. WICKHAM
Did you see him while you were at Lambton?

ELIZABETH
Yes, he introduced us to his sister.

MR. WICKHAM
And do you like her?

ELIZABETH
Very much.

MR. WICKHAM
I have heard that she is improved within this year.

ELIZABETH
I dare say she will; she has got over a most trying time.

MR. WICKHAM
Did you go by the village of Kymptom? I mention it because
that is the living I ought to have had.

ELIZABETH

How should you have liked making sermons?

MR. WICKHAM

Exceedingly well.

ELIZABETH

I did hear, that there was a time when you actually declared your resolution of never taking orders.

(**MR. WICKHAM** is obviously uncomfortable.
ELIZABETH notes his discomfort.)

Come, Mr. Wickham, we are brother and sister. Do not let us quarrel about the past. I hope we shall always be of one mind.

(**ELIZABETH** holds out her hand. **MR. WICKHAM** kisses it and then walks away.)

(BLACKOUT)

ACT II

Scene 8

SETTING: The Bennet parlor.

AT RISE: ELIZABETH and JANE are present.

JANE
It was wonderful to see Lydia again. Now we will not see her nor Wickham again for two or three years. It will be hard on our mother.

ELIZABETH
Give her but another week and something else will distract her.

(**MARY** and **KITTY** enter. **KITTY** is very excited.)

KITTY
Jane! Elizabeth You will never guess. Mr. Bingley is come to Netherfield.

ELIZABETH
What?

KITTY
Truly, for we heard it from our Aunt Philips, whom we met in Meryton. Isn't that right, Mary?

MARY
I know not, for I was looking at the bookseller's window.

KITTY
He came down yesterday.

ELIZABETH
What do you think, Jane?

JANE
I assure you that the news does not affect me without pleasure or pain. It is hard that a man cannot come to a house which he has legally hired, without all this speculation.

> (There is the sound of horses. **KITTY** runs to the window.)

KITTY
Mama! Mr. Bingley is riding towards the house.

> (**MRS. BENNET** enters.)

MRS. BENNET
What! Let me see.
> (She looks out the window.)
Oh! Jane! He is here.

KITTY
There is a gentleman with him. It looks like that man that used to be here with him. Mr. – what's his name – that tall, proud man.

MRS. BENNET
Good gracious! Mr. Darcy! So it is. Well, any friend of Mr. Bingley's will always be welcome here; but I must say I hate the sight of him.

> (They all try to appear nonchalant when **HILL** enters, followed by the **MR. BINGLEY** and **MR. DARCY**.)

HILL
> (Curtsies.)

Mr. Bingley and Mr. Darcy.
                    (**HILL** exits as the men enter. Bows/curtsies.)

MRS. BENNET
Mr. Bingley, it is so good to see you again. Mr. Darcy.

MR. BINGLEY
Mrs. Bennet, it is good to see you – and your family – again.
                    (They all sit.)

MRS. BENNET
It is a long time since you went away and a great many
changes have happened. Miss Lucas is married, as is one of
my own daughters. You must have seen it in the papers,
though it was not as it ought to be. It only said, 'Lately
George Wickham to Miss Lydia Bennet.' And now they are
gone to the north and there they are to stay. I suppose you
have heard of his joining the regiment there. Thank heaven
he has *some* friends, though perhaps, not as many as he
deserves.

ELIZABETH
                    (Embarrassed.)
How is your sister, Mr. Darcy?

MR. DARCY
She is well, thank you, Miss Bennet.

ELIZABETH
Is she still at Pemberley?

MR. DARCY
Yes, she remains there until Christmas.

ELIZABETH
Pray, give her my regards when next you see her.

MR. DARCY

I will.

JANE

And your sisters, Mr. Bingley, are they come down with you?

MR. BINGLEY

My sisters chose to stay in town as Darcy and I are come to
Netherfield to shoot.
(Stands.)
But now, Darcy and I must take our leave.

MRS. BENNET

So soon? Well, thank you for coming. You must come to take
supper with us, Mr. Bingley... And your friend. And when you
have killed all your own birds, Mr. Bingley, I beg you will
come here and shoot as many Mr. Bennet's birds as you
please.

MR. BINGLEY

Thank you. We shall. Good afternoon.

> (Ad lib goodbyes; bows/curtsies. **MR.
> BINGLEY** and **MR. DARCY** exit. **MRS.
> BENNET** sits down. **JANE** and
> **ELIZABETH** cross to the window to watch
> them leave.)

JANE

(Quietly to **ELIZABETH**.)

Now that this first meeting is over, I feel perfectly easy. I
shall never be embarrassed again by his coming. It will then
be publicly seen, that on both sides we met only as common
and indifferent acquaintance.

ELIZABETH

Yes, very indifferent indeed.

(Laughs softly.)
Oh Jane, take care. I think you are in very great danger of making him as much in love with you as ever.

(BLACKOUT)

ACT II

Scene 9

SETTING: The Bennet parlor.

AT RISE: **MR. BINGLEY** is sitting with **MRS. BENNET**, **JANE, ELIZABETH**, and **KITTY**.

MRS. BENNET

It was nice of you to call on us again, Mr. Bingley. Pray, have some more tea cake. You say Mr. Darcy is gone?

> (**MRS. BENNET** continually winks at **KITTY** and **ELIZABETH. ELIZABETH** does not look at her.)

MR. BINGLEY

He had business that required his attention.

MRS. BENNET

I see.

KITTY

What is the matter, Mama? What do you keep winking at me for?

MRS. BENNET

Nonsense, Kitty. I did not wink at you... Now that you mention it, however, I do have something to say to you. Come.

> (**MRS. BENNET** and **KITTY** begin to exit; she turns back.)

Lizzy, my dear, I want to speak with you as well.

> (**ELIZABETH** follows reluctantly. All three women exit and stand outside the door. Inside the room, **MR. BINGLEY** gets down on one knee and holds **JANE'S** hand. He mouths a

proposal.)

ELIZABETH
Mama, I do not know why we are out here.

MRS. BENNET
I know what I am doing. We may as well leave them by
themselves. Kitty and I are going up stairs to my room.

ELIZABETH
I'm sure that Jane would wish me to stay with her.

MRS. BENNET
And I'm sure Mr. Bingley would wish you not. A little more
will do the trick. Come, Kitty.

> (**MRS. BENNET** and **KITTY** exit.
> **ELIZABETH** waits a moment and then opens
> the door to find **MR. BINGLEY** standing near
> **JANE.**)

ELIZABETH
I beg your pardon.
> (**ELIZABETH** starts to leave.)

JANE
No, Lizzy, wait.
> (**JANE** whispers something to **MR.**
> **BINGLEY**, who smiles and leaves the room.
> **JANE** looks at **ELIZABETH**, holds out a
> hand and smiles.)

It is too much! I do not deserve it. Oh, why is not everybody as
happy?

ELIZABETH
Jane!

JANE

He loves me! He still loves me. I am so happy! He has gone to my father. I am certainly the most fortunate creature that ever existed. That I should bring such pleasure to all my dear family. If I could but see you as happy.

ELIZABETH

If you were to give me forty such men I could never be so happy. Till I have your goodness, I can never have your happiness. Perhaps, if I have very good luck, I may meet with another Mr. Collins in time.

(They laugh.)

(**MR.** and **MRS. BENNET** enter. Ad lib hugs and excitement.)

MR. BENNET

Jane, I congratulate you. You will be a very happy woman.

JANE

Thank you, Father.

MR. BENNET

You are a good girl and I have great pleasure in thinking you so happily settled. I have not a doubt of your doing very well together. You are both so complying, that nothing will ever be resolved. So easy that every servant will cheat you. And so generous that you will always exceed your income.

MRS. BENNET

Exceed their income! My dear Mr. Bennet, what are you thinking of? Why, he has four or five thousand a year.

MR. BENNET

Come with me, Jane. I believe there is a young man in my study who wished to talk with you.

(**MR. BENNET** and **JANE** exit.)

HILL
(Enters and curtsies.)
Lady Catherine DeBourgh.
(**HILL** exits.)

(All stand and curtsey as **LADY
CATHERINE** enters. **LADY CATHERINE**
says nothing, but looks around and then sits.
After a moment she speaks.)

LADY CATHERINE
That, I suppose, is your mother?

ELIZABETH
Yes, ma'am. Lady Catherine, this is my mother, Mrs. Bennet.

LADY CATHERINE
This is a most inconvenient sitting room. The windows face
full west.

MRS. BENNET
We never sit in this room until after dinner.

LADY CATHERINE
(Stands. **MRS. BENNET** and **ELIZABETH**
stand.)
Mrs. Bennet, if you will excuse us, I have something to
discuss with your daughter.

MRS. BENNET
Yes, of course, I will go and see about tea.
(**MRS. BENNET** exits.)

LADY CATHERINE
You can be at no loss, Miss Bennet to understand the reason for my journey.

ELIZABETH
Indeed, you are mistaken, ma'am. I have not been able to account for the honor of seeing you here.

LADY CATHERINE
Miss Bennet, I am not to be trifled with. A report of a most alarming nature reached me two days ago. I was told, that not only was your sister on the point of being most advantageously married, but that you, would in all likelihood, be united to my nephew, Mr. Darcy. I knew it must be a scandalous falsehood and resolved on setting off for this place, that I might make my sentiments known to you.

ELIZABETH
If you believed it to be impossible to be true, I wonder you took the trouble of coming so far. What could your Ladyship propose by it?

LADY CATHERINE
To insist upon having such a report universally contradicted.

ELIZABETH
Your coming to Longbourn, to see me and my family, will be a confirmation, if indeed such a report is in existence.

LADY CATHERINE
If! Can you declare that there is no foundation for it?

ELIZABETH
I do not pretend to possess equal frankness with your Ladyship. You may ask questions, which I shall not choose to answer.

LADY CATHERINE

This is not to be borne, Miss Bennet. I insist on being
satisfied. Has my nephew made you an offer of marriage?

ELIZABETH

Your Ladyship has declared it to be impossible.

LADY CATHERINE

It ought to be so. But your arts and allurements may have
made him forget what he owes to himself and to his family.

ELIZABETH

If I have, I shall be the last person to confess it.

LADY CATHERINE

Miss Bennet, do you know who I am? I have not been
accustomed to such language as this. I am almost the nearest
relation he has and am entitled to know all his dearest
concerns.

ELIZABETH

But you are not entitled to know mine, nor will such behavior
as this ever induce me to be explicit.

LADY CATHERINE

Let me be rightly understood. This match, to which you have
the presumption to aspire, can never take place. Mr. Darcy is
engaged to my daughter. Now, what have you to say?

ELIZABETH

Only this, that if he is so, you can have no reason to suppose
he will make an offer to me.

LADY CATHERINE

The engagement between them is of a peculiar kind. From
their infancy, it was the favorite wish of his mother as well as
hers. If you willfully act against the inclinations of family, do

not expect to be noticed by his family or friends. Your alliance will be a disgrace.

ELIZABETH

These would be a heavy misfortune indeed. But the wife of Mr. Darcy must have such extraordinary happiness that she could have no cause to repine.

LADY CATHERINE

Is this to be endured? If you were sensible of your own good, you would not quit the sphere to which you were brought up.

ELIZABETH

In marrying your nephew, I should not be quitting that sphere. He is a gentleman, I am a gentleman's daughter. So far we are equal.

LADY CATHERINE

But who was your mother? Who are your uncles and aunts? Do not imagine me ignorant of their condition.

ELIZABETH

Whatever my connections may be, if your nephew does not object to them, they can be nothing to you.

LADY CATHERINE

Tell me, once for all, are you engaged to him?

ELIZABETH

... I am not.

LADY CATHERINE
(Relieved.)

And will you promise me never to enter into such an engagement?

ELIZABETH

I will make no promise of the kind.
> (**ELIZABETH** turns to exit.)

LADY CATHERINE

Not so hasty, if you please. I have another objection. I am no stranger to the particulars of your youngest sister's infamous elopement. I know it all. Is *such* a girl to be my nephew's sister? Are the shades of Pemberley to be thus polluted?

ELIZABETH

You can have nothing further to say. You have insulted me in every possible method.

LADY CATHERINE

You have no regard, then, for the honor of my nephew? Unfeeling, selfish girl! You are resolved to have him?

ELIZABETH

I am only resolved to act in the manner which will constitute my happiness, without reference to you or to any person so wholly unconnected with me.

LADY CATHERINE

And this is your final resolve. Very well. I shall now know how to act. I take no leave of you, Miss Bennet, I send no compliments to your mother. You deserve no such attention. I am most seriously displeased.

> (**LADY CATHERINE** exits. **ELIZABETH** sits and stares until **MR. BENNET** enters.)

MR. BENNET

Lizzy, I was going to look for you. I have just received a letter from Mr. Collins that astonished me.

ELIZABETH
Mr. Collins! What can he have to say?

MR. BENNET
He begins by congratulating me on the approaching nuptials
of my eldest daughter. Then he goes on, "and your daughter,
Elizabeth, it is presumed, will not long bear the name Bennet,
and the young gentlemen may be looked upon as one of the
most illustrious in the land." Have you any idea, Lizzy who
this gentlemen is? But now it comes out, "I have reason to
believe that his aunt, Lady Catherine DeBourgh, does not
look on the match with a friendly eye."

Mr. Darcy, you see is the man. Mr. Darcy, who never looks
upon a woman but to see a blemish. Is it not admirable?

ELIZABETH
(Attempts a slight laugh.)
Yes, it is.

MR. BENNET
And now Lady Catherine herself comes for a visit... But,
Lizzy, you look as if you did not enjoy it. I hope you are not
affronted at an idle report. For what do we live for, but to
make sport for our neighbors and laugh at them in our turn?

(BLACKOUT)

ACT II

Scene 10

SETTING: The Bennet parlor.

AT RISE: **ELIZABETH** is sitting, reading, when
                JANE enters with **MR. DARCY** and **MR. BINGLEY**.

ELIZABETH
Oh; Mr. Bingley. Mr. Darcy.
                (Bows/curtsies.)
Mr. Darcy? I did not realize you were come to Netherfield. I
understood you were in town.

MR. DARCY
Yes, I had business that required my attention. I returned
just this morning.

JANE
Mr. Bingley has suggested we all walk to Meryton.

ELIZABETH
Oh...that would be nice.

                (**JANE** and **MR. BINGLEY** exit.
                ELIZABETH begins to follow but turns to
                MR. DARCY.)

ELIZABETH
I have been most anxious to thank you for your kindness to
my sister and my family. Lydia's thoughtlessness first
betrayed it to me and I could not rest 'til I knew the
particulars.

MR. DARCY
If you will thank me, let it be for yourself alone. Much as I

respect your family, I thought only of you.

(He stops her.)

You are too generous to trifle with me. If your feelings are still what they were last April, tell me so at once. My affections are unchanged; but one word from you will silence me on this subject forever.

ELIZABETH

My feelings. They are most definitely changed from what I felt. They are, in fact, quite the opposite.

MR. DARCY

My aunt called on me and told me of her recent visit to you. Unfortunately, the effect of her visit was contrary to what she wished. It taught me to hope, for I knew enough of you to be certain that had you been decided against me, you would have acknowledged it to Lady Catherine.

ELIZABETH

(Laughs.)

Yes, you know enough of my frankness to believe me capable of that. After abusing you so abominably to your face, I could have no scruples in abusing you to your relations.

MR. DARCY

What did you say that I did not deserve? My behavior at that time merited the severest reproof. "Had you behaved in a more gentleman-like manner." I cannot think of it without abhorrence.

ELIZABETH

Oh, do not repeat what I said. I have long been most heartily ashamed of it.

MR. DARCY

As a child, although I had good parents, I was encouraged to care for none beyond my own circle. Such I might still have been but for you. By you, I was properly humbled. I came to you without a doubt of my reception. You showed me how insufficient were all my pretensions to please a woman worthy of being pleased. And so now I ask you once again, dearest, loveliest Elizabeth, will you marry me?

ELIZABETH
How could I not? You have uncovered my heart.
(They embrace and kiss.)

(CURTAIN)

7599892R00078

Printed in Great Britain
by Amazon.co.uk, Ltd.,
Marston Gate.